SELECTED

POEMS

Rita Dove

SELECTED

POEMS

Pantheon Books
New York

811
DOV

For my family—

and with special thanks to Gerald Costanzo,
small press architect and book builder
who gave these poems their first home.

Contents

SELECTED

POEMS

Introduction

When I am asked: "What made you want to be a writer?" my answer has always been: "Books." First and foremost, now, then, and always, I have been passionate about books. From the time I began to read, as a child, I loved to feel their heft in my hand and the warm spot caused by their intimate weight in my lap; I loved the crisp whisper of a page turning, the musky odor of old paper and the sharp inky whiff of new pages. Leather bindings sent me into ecstasy. I even loved to gaze at a closed book and daydream about the possibilities inside—it was like contemplating a genie's lamp. Of course, my favorite fairy tale was *A Thousand and One Nights*—imagine buying your life with stories!—and my favorite cartoons were those where animated characters popped out of books and partied while the unsuspecting humans slept. In books, I could travel anywhere, be anybody, understand worlds long past and imaginary colonies in the future. My idea of a bargain was to go to the public library, wander along the bookshelves, and emerge with a chin-high stack of books that were mine, all mine, for two weeks—free of charge!

What I remember most about long summer days is browsing the bookshelves in our solarium to see if there were any new additions. I grew up with those rows of books; I knew where each one was shelved and immediately spotted newcomers. And after months had gone by and there'd be no new books, I would think: Okay, I guess I'll try this one—and then discover that the very book I had been avoiding because of a drab cover or small print was actually a wonderful read. Louis Untermeyer's *Treasury of Best Loved Poems* had a sickeningly sweet lilac and gold cover and was forbiddingly thick, but I finally pulled it off the shelf and discovered a cornucopia of emotional and linguistic delights, from "The Ballad of Barbara Fritchie," which I adored for its sheer length and rather numbing rhymes, to Langston Hughes's dazzlingly syncopated "Dream Boogie." Then there was Shakespeare—daunting for many years because it was his entire oeuvre, in matching wine-red volumes that were so thick they looked more like over-sized bouillon cubes than books, and yet it was that ponderous title—*The Complete Works of William Shakespeare*—that enticed me, because here was a lifetime's work—a lifetime!—in two compact, dense packages. I began with the long poem "The Rape of

Lucrece," looking for the rape, of course (which I didn't find); I sampled a few sonnets, which I found beautiful but rather adult; and finally wandered into the plays—first *Romeo and Juliet,* then *Macbeth, Julius Caesar, A Midsummer Night's Dream, Twelfth Night*—enthralled by the language, by the fact that poetry was spinning the story. Of course I did not understand every single word, but I was too young to know that this was supposed to be difficult; besides, no one was waiting to test me on anything, so, free from pressure, I dove in.

At the same time, my brother, two years my senior, had become a science fiction buff, so I'd read his *Analog* and *Fantasy and Science Fiction* magazines after he was finished with them. One story particularly fascinated me: A retarded boy in a small town begins building a sculpture in his backyard, using old and discarded materials—coke bottles, scrap iron, string, and bottle caps. Everyone laughs at him, but he continues building. Then one day he disappears. And when the neighbors investigate, they discover that the sculpture has been dragged onto the back porch and that the screen door is open. Somehow the narrator of the story figures out how to switch on the sculpture: The back door frame begins to glow, and when he steps through it, he's in an alternate universe, a town the mirror image of his own—even down to the colors, with green roses and an orange sky. And he walks through this town until he comes to the main square, where there is a statue erected to—who else?—the village idiot.

I loved this story, the idea that the dreamy, mild, scatter-brained boy of one world could be the hero of another. And in a way, I identified with that village idiot because in real life I was painfully shy and awkward; the place where I felt most alive was between the pages of a book.

Although I loved books, for a long time I had no aspirations to be a writer. The possibility was beyond my imagination. I liked to write, however—and on long summer days when I ran out of reading material or my legs had fallen asleep because I had been curled up on the couch for hours on end, I made up my own stories. Most were abandoned midway. Those that I did bring to a conclusion I neither showed to others nor considered saving.

My first piece of writing I thought enough of to keep was a novel called *Chaos,* which was about robots taking over the earth. I had just entered third or fourth grade; the novel had forty-three chapters, and each chapter was twenty lines or less because I used each week's spelling list as the basis for each chapter, and there were twenty words per list. In the course of the year I wrote one installment per week, and I never knew what was going to happen next—the words led me, not the other way around.

At that time I didn't think of writing as an activity people admitted doing. I had no living role models—a "real" writer was a long-dead white male, usually with a white beard to match. Much later, when I was in eleventh grade, my English teacher, Miss Oechsner, took me to a book-signing in a downtown hotel. She didn't ask me if I'd like to go—she asked my parents instead, signed me and a classmate (who is now a professor of literature) out of school one day, and took us to meet a writer. The writer was John Ciardi, a poet who also had translated Dante's *Divine Comedy,* which I had heard of, vaguely. At that moment I realized that writers were real people and how it was possible to write down a poem or story in the intimate sphere of one's own room and then share it with the world.

I wrote the poems in this book between the mid-seventies and mid-eighties, well after that revelation, but certainly propelled by it. I often wonder, had I not gone to that book-signing, if eventually I would have found myself exploring the world through language anyway. This is no moot speculation; each of us would have taken a different path in our life with little effort on our own if all the roadblocks and unmarked junctures we encounter constantly had assumed a slightly different constellation. The mystery of destiny boils down to the ultimate—and ultimately unanswerable—questions: How does where I come from determine where I've ended up? Why am I what I am and not what I thought I'd be? What did I think I'd be? Where do I reside most completely?

From time to time in my poetry I have tried to sidle up to the answers, to eavesdrop on the gods. My attempts often reach back to childhood, with its volatile pleasures and profound trepidations. Whenever I make this trip, via the air bridge of memory, I find that there is always some disclosure, some *connection,* waiting to be seen—more precisely, waiting to be articulated. So it happened that, in the middle of the unexpected but exhilarating turmoil of this spring, I found myself writing a poem about the old neighborhood—its physical topography as well as the spiritual and aesthetical terrain—and, to conclude this introduction, I'd like to quote it here in its entirety:

In the Old Neighborhood

> To *pull yourself up by your own roots;*
> *to eat the last meal in your own neighborhood.*
> —*Adrienne Rich, "Shooting Script"*

Raccoons have invaded the crawl space
of my sister's bridal apartment.
The landlord insists they're squirrels;
squirrels he'll fight, not raccoons—
too ferocious and faggy, licking
their black-gloved paws.

My mother works up a sudsbath
of worries: what if
the corsages are too small,
if the candles
accidentally ignite
the reverend's sleeve?

Father prefers a more
reticent glory. He consoles
his roses—dusts them
with fungicide, spades in
fortified earth. Each summer
he brandishes color
over the neighborhood,
year after year producing
lovelier mutants: these
bruised petticoats, for instance,
or this sudden teacup
blazing empty, its rim
a drunken red smear.

I am indoors, pretending
to read today's paper
as I had been taught
twenty years before:
headlines first,
lead story (continued on A-14),
followed by editorials and

local coverage. Even then
I never finished, snared
between datelines—*Santiago,
Paris, Dakar*—names as
unreal as the future
even now.

My brother rummages upstairs;
I skip to the daily horoscope.
I've read every book in this house,
I know which shelf to go to
to taste crumbling saltines
(*don't eat with your nose in a book!*)
and the gritty slick of sardines,
silted bones of no consequence
disintegrating on the tongue. . . .

That was *Romeo and Juliet,*
strangely enough, and just as odd
stuffed green olives
for a premature attempt at *The Iliad.*
Candy buttons went with Brenda Starr,
Bazooka bubble gum with the Justice
League of America. Fig Newtons
and *King Lear,* bitter lemon as well
for Othello, that desolate
conspicuous soul.
But Macbeth demanded dry bread,
crumbs brushed from a lap
as I staggered off the cushions
contrite, having read far past
my mother's calling.

The rummaging's stopped. Well,
he's found it, whatever it was.
Bee vomit, he said once,
that's all honey is, so that
I could not put my tongue to its
jellied flame without tasting
regurgitated blossoms.
In revenge, I would explicate
the strawberry:

how each select seed
chose to breed in darkness,
the stomach's cauldron
brewing a host of vines
trained to climb and snap
a windpipe shut—then
watched my brother's eyes as
Mom sliced the red hearts into sugar
and left them to build their own
improbable juice.

I fold the crossword away,
walk back to the kitchen where
she's stacked platters high
with chicken and silvery cabbage.
Lean at the sink, listen to her chatter
while the pressure cooker ticks
whole again whole again now.

Out where the maple tree
used to stand
there once was a tent
(official Eagle Scout issue):
inside a young girl
weeping and her brother
twitching with bravado
because their father, troop leader
in the pitched dark,
insisted they'd love it by morning.

(Let me go back to the white rock
on the black lawn, the number
stenciled in negative light.
Let me return to the shadow
of a house moored in moonlight,
gables pitched bright above
the extinguished grass,

and stalk the hushed perimeter,
roses closed around their scent,
azaleas dissembling behind the garage

and the bugeyed pansies
leaning over, inquisitive,
in their picketed beds.

What are these, I'll ask, stooping
to lift the pale leaves, and these?
Weeds, my father mutters
from his pillow. *All weeds.*)

Chink. Chink. Sound made by
a starling the first hot morning
in June, when Dad switched on
the attic fan and nothing
stirred—faraway then
a *chink-chip-shiver,*
whittled breath of a bird
caught in the blades.

We each dropped our books
and ran to identify
the first tragedy of the season:
baby sister run down
or a pebbly toad
the lawn mower had shuffled
into liver canapes—
each of us thinking
At least I'm not the one.
Who could guess it would be
a bird with no song,
no plumage worth stopping for?
Who could think up a solution
this anonymous, a switch
flipped on reverse
to blow the feathers out?

"—tea roses, I'd say, plus
a few carnations—and baby's breath,
of course. Are ferns
too much?" I am back
again, matron of honor,
firstborn daughter nodding *yes*

as I wrap bones and eggshells
into old newspaper for burning,
folding the corners in
properly,
as I had been taught to do.

(Charlottesville, Virginia, June 1993)

THE
YELLOW
HOUSE
ON
THE
CORNER

I

This Life

The green lamp flares on the table.
You tell me the same thing
as that one,
asleep, upstairs.
Now I see: the possibilities
are golden dresses in a nutshell.

As a child, I fell in love
with a Japanese woodcut
of a girl gazing at the moon.
I waited with her for her lover.
He came in white breeches and sandals.
He had a goatee—he had

your face, though I didn't know it.
Our lives will be the same—
your lips, swollen from whistling
at danger,
and I a stranger
in this desert,
nursing the tough skins of figs.

The Bird Frau

When the boys came home, everything stopped
the way he left it—her apron, the back stairs,
the sun losing altitude over France
as the birds scared up from the fields,
a whirring curtain of flak—

                Barmherzigkeit!
her son, her man. She went inside, fed the parakeet,
broke its neck. Spaetzle bubbling on the stove,
windchimes tinkling above the steam, her face
in the hall mirror, bloated, a heart.
Let everything go wild!

                Blue jays, crows!
She hung suet from branches, the air quick
around her head with tiny spastic machinery
—starlings, finches—her head a crown of feathers.
She ate less, grew lighter, air tunnelling
through bone, singing

                a small song.
"Ein Liedchen, Kinder!" The children ran away.
She moved about the yard like an old rag bird.
Still at war, she rose at dawn, watching out
for Rudi, come home on crutches,
the thin legs balancing his atom of life.

Robert Schumann, Or: Musical Genius Begins with Affliction

It began with *A*—years before in a room
with a white piano and lyre-back chairs,
Schumann panted on a whore on a coverlet
and the oboe got its chance . . .

It never stops: the alarm
going off in his head is a cry
in a thicket of its own making.
Cello Concerto in A minor,

Symphony in A, Phantasiestücke,
Concerto for Piano and Orchestra
in A minor, Opus 54: the notes
stack themselves onto the score-sheets

like unfamiliar furniture, the music
pulls higher and higher, and still
each phrase returns to *A*
no chord is safe from *A*

Years before, in a room with delicate chairs,
he was happy. There were no wretched sounds.
He was Adam naked in creation,
starting over as the sky rained apples.

Happenstance

When you appeared it was as if
magnets cleared the air.
I had never seen that smile before
or your hair, flying silver. Someone
waving goodbye, she was silver, too.
Of course you didn't see me.
I called softly so you could choose
not to answer—then called again.
You turned in the light, your eyes
seeking your name.

Small Town

Someone is sitting in the red house.
There is no way of telling who it is, although
the woman, indistinct, in the doorway must know;
and the man in the chestnut tree
who wields the binoculars
does not wish to be seen from the window.

The paint was put there by a previous owner.
The dog in the flower bed
is bound by indiscriminate love,
which is why he does not bark
and why in one of the darkened rooms
someone sits, a crackling vacuum.

The woman wears a pale blue nightgown
and stares vaguely upward. The man,
whose form appears clearly among the leaves,
is not looking at her
so much as she at him,
while away behind the town a farmer
weeps, plowing his fields by night
to avoid being laughed at during the day.

The Snow King

In a far far land where men are men
And women are sun and sky,
The snow king paces. And light throws
A gold patina on the white spaces
Where sparrows lie frozen in hallways.

And he weeps for the sparrows, their clumped feathers:
Where is the summer that lasts forever,
The night as soft as antelope eyes?
The snow king roams the lime-filled spaces,
His cracked heart a slow fire, a garnet.

Sightseeing

Come here, I want to show you something.
I inquired about the church yesterday:

the inner courtyard, also in ruin, has been left
exactly as the villagers found it

after the Allies left. What a consort
of broken dolls! Look, they were mounted

at the four corners of the third floor terrace
and the impact from the cobblestones

snapped off wings and other appendages.
The heads rolled the farthest. Someone

started to pile the limbs together—
from the weight of the pieces, an adult—

a deserter, perhaps, or a distraught priest.
Whoever it was, the job was interrupted,

so to speak, in mid-step: this forearm
could not have fallen so far from its owner

without assistance. The villagers,
come here to give thanks, took one look in

and locked the gates: "A terrible sign . . ."
But all this palaver about symbols and

"the ceremony of innocence drowned" is—
as you and I know—civilization's way

of manufacturing hope. Let's look
at the facts. Forget they are children of angels

and they become childish monsters.
Remember, and an arm gracefully upraised

is raised not in anger but a mockery of gesture.
The hand will hold both of mine. The vulgarity

of life in exemplary size is why
we've come to regard this abandoned

constellation, and why two drunks
would walk all the way crosstown

to look at a bunch of smashed statues.

Upon Meeting Don L. Lee, In a Dream

He comes toward me with lashless eyes,
Always moving in the yellow half-shadows.
From his mouth I know he has never made love
To thin white boys in toilet stalls . . .

Among the trees, the black trees,
Women in robes stand, watching. They begin
To chant, stamping their feet in wooden cadences
As they stretch their beaded arms to him;

Moments slip by like worms.
"Seven years ago . . ." he begins; but
I cut him off: "Those years are gone—
What is there now?" He starts to cry; his eyeballs

Burst into flame. I can see caviar
Imbedded like buckshot between his teeth.
His hair falls out in clumps of burned-out wire.
The music grows like branches in the wind.

I lie down, chuckling as the grass curls around me.
He can only stand, fists clenched, and weep
Tears of iodine, while the singers float away,
Rustling on brown paper wings.

"Teach Us to Number Our Days"

In the old neighborhood, each funeral parlor
is more elaborate than the last.
The alleys smell of cops, pistols bumping their thighs,
each chamber steeled with a slim blue bullet.

Low-rent balconies stacked to the sky.
A boy plays tic-tac-toe on a moon
crossed by TV antennae, dreams

he has swallowed a blue bean.
It takes root in his gut, sprouts
and twines upward, the vines curling
around the sockets and locking them shut.

And this sky, knotting like a dark tie?
The patroller, disinterested, holds all the beans.

August. The mums nod past, each a prickly heart on a sleeve.

Nigger Song: An Odyssey

We six pile in, the engine churning ink:
We ride into the night.
Past factories, past graveyards
And the broken eyes of windows, we ride
Into the gray-green nigger night.

We sweep past excavation sites; the pits
Of gravel gleam like mounds of ice.
Weeds clutch at the wheels;
We laugh and swerve away, veering
Into the black entrails of the earth,
The green smoke sizzling on our tongues . . .

In the nigger night, thick with the smell of cabbages,
Nothing can catch us.
Laughter spills like gin from glasses,
And "yeah" we whisper, "yeah"
We croon, "yeah."

II

Five Elephants

are walking towards me.
When morning is still a frozen
tear in the brain, they come
from the east, trunk to tail,
clumsy ballerinas.

How to tell them all evening
I refused consolation? Five umbrellas, five
willows, five bridges and their shadows!
They lift their trunks, hooking the sky
I would rush into, split

pod of quartz and lemon. I could say
they are five memories, but
that would be unfair.
Rather pebbles seeking refuge in the heart.
They move past me. I turn and follow,

and for hours we meet no one else.

Geometry

I prove a theorem and the house expands:
the windows jerk free to hover near the ceiling,
the ceiling floats away with a sigh.

As the walls clear themselves of everything
but transparency, the scent of carnations
leaves with them. I am out in the open

and above the windows have hinged into butterflies,
sunlight glinting where they've intersected.
They are going to some point true and unproven.

Champagne

The natives here have given up their backyards
and are happy living where we cannot see them.
No shade! The sky insists upon its blueness,
the baskets their roped ovals.
Gravel blinds us, blurring the road's shoulders.
Figures moving against the corduroyed hills
are not an industry to speak of, just
an alchemy whose yield is pleasure.

Come quickly—a whiff of yeast
means bubbles are forming, trapped
by sugar and air. The specialist who turns
30,000 bottles a day 10° to the right
lines up in a vaulted cellar
for an Italian red at the end of the day.
On either side for as far as we can see,
racks of unmarked bottles lying in cool fever.

Three centuries before in this dim corridor
a monk paused to sip, said it pricked
the tongue like stars. When we emerge
it is as difficult to remember the monk
as it is to see things as they are:
houses waver in the heat, stone walls
blaze. The hurt we feel is delicate—
all for ourselves and all for nothing.

Night Watch

In this stucco house there is nothing but air.
The Mexican sky shivers toward morning.
I am on the four-star vacation from the wings
Of man to these halls draped in heavy matting
Where lizards hang from light fixtures.
From an invisible courtyard comes
The broken applause of castanets.

Romance may lurk in the land of white orchids,
But no slim-hipped Latin comes for me.
Coated servants scuttle through the halls.
I hear the morning wind around the house
As the light goes out
To the shanties in the mountains.

The Secret Garden

I was ill, lying on my bed of old papers,
when you came with white rabbits in your arms;
and the doves scattered upwards, flying to mothers,
and the snails sighed under their baggage of stone . . .

Now your tongue grows like celery between us:
Because of our love-cries, cabbage darkens in its nest;
the cauliflower thinks of her pale, plump children
and turns greenish-white in a light like the ocean's.

I was sick, fainting in the smell of teabags,
when you came with tomatoes, a good poetry.
I am being wooed. I am being conquered
by a cliff of limestone that leaves chalk on my breasts.

A Suite for Augustus

1963

That winter I stopped loving the President
And loved his dying. He smiled
From his frame on the chifferobe
And watched as I reined in each day
Using buttons for rosary beads.

Then tapwater rinsed orange through my underwear.
You moved away, and in tall white buildings
Typed speeches, each word-cluster a satellite,
A stone cherry that arced over the violent bay,
Broadcasting ball games and good will to Cuba . . .

But to me, stretched out under percale,
The cherry blinks sadly: Goodbye, goodbye,
Spinning into space. In this black place
I touch the doorknobs of my knees, begging to open
Me, an erector set, spilled and unpuzzled.

D.C.

1
Roosters corn wooden dentures
pins & thimbles embroidery hoops
greenbacks & silver snuff & silver

brontosaurus bones couched on Smithsonian velvet

2
A bloodless finger pointing to heaven, you say,
is surely no more impossible than this city:
A no man's land, a capital askew,
a postcard framed by imported blossoms—
and now this outrageous cue stick
lying, reflected, on a black table.

3
Leaving his chair under the giant knee-cap,
he prowls the edge of the prune-black water.
Down the lane of clipped trees, a ghost trio
plays Dixie. His slaves have outlived him
in this life, too. Harmonicas breathe in,
the gray palms clap: "De broomstick's jumped, the world's
not wide."

Planning the Perfect Evening

I keep him waiting, tuck in the curtains,
buff my nails (such small pink eggshells).
As if for the last time, I descend the stair.

He stands penguin-stiff in a room
that's so quiet we forget it is there.
Now nothing, not even breath, can come

between us, not even the aroma of punch
and sneakers as we dance the length
of the gymnasium and crepe paper streams

down like cartoon lightning. Ah,
Augustus, where did you learn to samba?
And what is that lump below your cummerbund?

Stardust. The band folds up
resolutely, with plum-dark faces.
The night still chirps. Sixteen cars

caravan to Georgia for a terrace,
beer and tacos. Even this far south
a thin blue ice shackles the moon,

and I'm happy my glass sizzles with stars.
How far away the world! And how hulking
you are, my dear, my sweet black bear!

Augustus Observes the Sunset

July. The conspiracy of colors—
Ketchup, marshmallows, the tub of ice,
Bacon strips floating in pale soup.
The sun, like a dragon spreading its tail,
Burns the blue air to ribbons.

Eastward, the corn swelling in its sockets,
A wall of silence, growing.
What are you doing in your own backyard
Holding your coat in your arms?
There's so much left to do!—You pack.
Above spareribs and snow-puffed potatoes
The sky shakes like a flag.

Wake

Stranded in the middle of the nation like this,
I turn eastward, following rivers.
My heart, shy mulatto, wanders toward
The salt-edged contours of rock and sand
That stretch ahead into darkness:

But you stand in the way, a young boy
Appearing on the bank of the Potomac,
Profile turned to sudden metal
And your shirt-front luminous
Under a thicket of cherry boughs.

You open your mouth as if to say
Tadpoles, pebbles,
Each word a droplet of creme de menthe.
What reaches me is not your words
But your breath, exalted and spearmint.

Back

Three years too late, I'm scholarshipped
to Europe and back.
Four years, a language later, and
your 39th jet lands in Kuwait.
(Down

through columns of khaki and ribbons,
escorted at night by the radiance
of oil fields, you relax at last—
goat milk and scotch, no women, no
maple trees. You think: how far I've come)

This barnstorming that led no closer to you
has stuffed my knees into violets,
buried me in the emerald hearts of leaves.
They are like twenty-mark bills, soft
dollars, they bring me back.

III

Belinda's Petition

(Boston, February, 1782)

To the honorable Senate and House
of Representatives of this Country,
new born: I am Belinda, an African,
since the age of twelve a Slave.
I will not take too much of your Time,
but to plead and place my pitiable Life
unto the Fathers of this Nation.

Lately your Countrymen have severed
the Binds of Tyranny. I would hope
you would consider the Same for me,
pure Air being the sole Advantage
of which I can boast in my present Condition.

As to the Accusation that I am Ignorant:
I received Existence on the Banks
of the Rio de Valta. All my Childhood
I expected nothing, if that be Ignorance.
The only Travelers were the Dead who returned
from the Ridge each Evening. How might
I have known of Men with Faces like the Moon,
who would ride toward me steadily for twelve Years?

The House Slave

The first horn lifts its arm over the dew-lit grass
and in the slave quarters there is a rustling—
children are bundled into aprons, cornbread

and water gourds grabbed, a salt pork breakfast taken.
I watch them driven into the vague before-dawn
while their mistress sleeps like an ivory toothpick

and Massa dreams of asses, rum and slave-funk.
I cannot fall asleep again. At the second horn,
the whip curls across the backs of the laggards—

sometimes my sister's voice, unmistaken, among them.
"Oh! pray," she cries. "Oh! pray!" Those days
I lie on my cot, shivering in the early heat,

and as the fields unfold to whiteness,
and they spill like bees among the fat flowers,
I weep. It is not yet daylight.

David Walker (1785–1830)

Free to travel, he still couldn't be shown how lucky
he was: *They strip and beat and drag us about*
like rattlesnakes. Home on Brattle Street, he took in the sign
on the door of the slop shop. All day at the counter—
white caps, ale-stained pea coats. Compass needles,
eloquent as tuning forks, shivered, pointing north.
Evenings, the ceiling fan sputtered like a second pulse.
Oh Heaven! I am full!! I can hardly move my pen!!!

On the faith of an eye-wink, pamphlets were stuffed
into trouser pockets. Pamphlets transported
in the coat linings of itinerant seamen, jackets
ringwormed with salt traded drunkenly to pursers
in the Carolinas, pamphlets ripped out, read aloud:
Men of colour, who are also of sense.
Outrage. Incredulity. Uproar in state legislatures.

We are the most wretched, degraded and abject set
of beings that ever lived since the world began.
The jewelled canaries in the lecture halls tittered,
pressed his dark hand between their gloves.
Every half-step was no step at all.
Every morning, the man on the corner strung a fresh
bunch of boots from his shoulders. "I'm happy!" he said.
"I never want to live any better or happier than
when I can get a-plenty of boots and shoes to clean!"

A second edition. A third.
The abolitionist press is *perfectly appalled.*
Humanity, kindness and the fear of the Lord
does not consist in protecting devils. A month—
his person (is that all?) found face-down
in the doorway at Brattle Street,
his frame slighter than friends remembered.

The Abduction

The bells, the cannons, the houses black with crepe,
all for the great Harrison! The citizenry of Washington
clotted the avenue—I among them, Solomon Northrup
from Saratoga Springs, free papers in my pocket, violin
under arm, my new friends Brown and Hamilton by my side.

Why should I have doubted them? The wages were good.
While Brown's tall hat collected pennies at the tent flap,
Hamilton's feet did a jig on a tightrope,
pigs squealed invisibly from the bleachers and I fiddled.

I remember how the windows rattled with each report.
Then the wine, like a pink lake, tipped.
I was lifted—the sky swivelled, clicked into place.

I floated on water I could not drink. Though the pillow
was stone, I climbed no ladders in that sleep.

I woke and found myself alone, in darkness and in chains.

The Transport of Slaves
From Maryland to Mississippi

(On August 22, 1839, a wagonload of slaves broke their chains, killed two white men, and would have escaped, had not a slave woman helped the Negro driver mount his horse and ride for help.)

I don't know if I helped him up
because I thought he was our salvation
or not. Left for dead in the middle
of the road, dust hovering around the body
like a screen of mosquitoes
shimmering in the hushed light.
The skin across his cheekbones
burst open like baked yams—
deliberate, the eyelids came apart—
his eyes were my eyes in a yellower face.
Death and salvation—one accommodates the other.
I am no brute. I got feelings.
He might have been a son of mine.

≈

"The Negro Gordon, barely escaping with his life, rode
into the plantation just as his pursuers came into sight.
The neighborhood was rallied and a search begun.
Some of the Negroes had taken to the woods but
were routed, ending this most shocking affray and murder."

≈

Eight miles south of Portsmouth, the last handcuff
broke clean from the skin. The last thing
the driver saw were the trees, improbable as broccoli,
before he was clubbed from behind. Sixty slaves
poured off the wagon, smelly, half-numb, free.

Baggage man Petit rushed in with his whip.
Some nigger's laid on another one's leg, he thought
before he saw they were loose. *Hold it!* he yelled;
but not even the wenches stopped. To his right
Atkins dropped under a crown of clubs. They didn't
even flinch. *Wait. You ain't supposed to act this way.*

Pamela

". . . the hour was come when the man must act, or forever be a slave."

At two, the barnyard settled
into fierce silence—anvil,
water pump glinted
as though everything waited
for the first step.
She stepped
into the open. The wind
lifted—behind her,
fields spread their sails.

There really is a star up there and moss on the trees. She
discovered if she kept a steady pace, she could walk forever.
The idea pleased her, and she hummed a hymn to herself—
Peach Point, Silk Hope, Beaver Bend. It seemed that the further
north she went, the freer she became. The stars were plates
for good meat; if she reached, they flashed and became coins.

White quiet. Night pushed over the hill.
The woods hiss with cockleburs,
each a small woolly head.
She feels old, older
than these friendly shadows
who, like the squirrels, don't come too near.
Knee-deep in muscadine, she watches them coming,
snapping the brush. They are
smiling, rifles crossed on their chests.

Someone's Blood

I stood at 6 a.m. on the wharf,
thinking: *This is Independence, Missouri.*
I am to stay here. The boat goes on to New Orleans.
My life seemed minutes old, and here it was ending.

I was silent, although she clasped me
and asked forgiveness for giving me life.
As the sun broke the water into a thousand needles
tipped with the blood from someone's finger,

the boat came gently apart from the wharf.
I watched till her face could not distinguish itself
from that shadow floated on broken sunlight.
I stood there. I could not help her. I forgive.

Cholera

At the outset, hysteria.
Destruction, the conjurers intoned.
Some dragged themselves off at night
to die in the swamp, to lie down
with the voices of mud and silk.

> *I know moonrise, I know starrise*

Against orders
the well and almost-well were assembled
and marched into the wood. When
a dry open place was found, halted.
The very weak got a piece of board
and fires were built, though the evening was warm.
Said the doctor, You'll live.

> *I walk in de moonlight, I walk in de*
> *starlight*

Who could say but that it wasn't anger
had to come out somehow? Pocketed filth.
The pouring-away of pints of pale fluid.

> *I'll walk in de graveyard, I'll walk*
> *through de graveyard*

Movement, dark and silken.
The dry-skinned conjurers circling the fire.
Here is pain, they whispered, and it is all ours.
Who would want to resist them?
By camplight their faces had taken on
the frail finality of ash.

> *I'll lie in de grave and stretch out my*
> *arms*

Well,
that was too much for the doctor.
Strip 'em! he ordered. And they
were slicked down with bacon fat and
superstition strapped from them
to the beat of the tam-tam. Those strong enough
rose up too, and wailed as they leapt.
It was a dance of unusual ferocity.

The Slave's Critique of
Practical Reason

Ain't got a reason
to run away—
leastways, not one
would save my life.
So I scoop speculation
into a hopsack.
I scoop fluff till
the ground rears white
and I'm the only dark
spot in the sky.

All day the children
sit in the weeds
to wait out the heat
with the rattlers.
All day Our Lady
of the Milk-Tooth
attends them
while I, the Owl
of the Broken Spirit
keep dipping and
thinking up tunes
that fly off quick
as they hit
the air. As far
as I can see,

it's hotter in heaven
than in the cool
cool earth. I know
'cause I've been there,
a stony mote
circling the mindless
blue, dropping rows
of little clouds,
no-good reasons
for sale.

Kentucky, 1833

It is Sunday, day of roughhousing. We are let out in the woods. The young boys wrestle and butt their heads together like sheep—a circle forms; claps and shouts fill the air. The women, brown and glossy, gather round the banjo player, or simply lie in the sun, legs and aprons folded. The weather's an odd monkey—any other day he's on our backs, his cotton eye everywhere; today the light sifts down like the finest cornmeal, coating our hands and arms with a dust. God's dust, old woman Acker says. She's the only one who could read to us from the Bible, before Massa forbade it. On Sundays, something hangs in the air, a hallelujah, a skitter of brass, but we can't call it by name and it disappears.

Then Massa and his gentlemen friends come to bet on the boys. They guffaw and shout, taking sides, red-faced on the edge of the boxing ring. There is more kicking, butting, and scuffling—the winner gets a dram of whiskey if he can drink it all in one swig without choking.

Jason is bucking and prancing about—Massa said his name reminded him of some sailor, a hero who crossed an ocean, looking for a golden cotton field. Jason thinks he's been born to great things—a suit with gold threads, vest and all. Now the winner is sprawled out under a tree and the sun, that weary tambourine, hesitates at the rim of the sky's green light. It's a crazy feeling that carries through the night; as if the sky were an omen we could not understand, the book that, if we could read, would change our lives.

IV

Adolescence—I

In water-heavy nights behind grandmother's porch
We knelt in the tickling grasses and whispered:
Linda's face hung before us, pale as a pecan,
And it grew wise as she said:
    "A boy's lips are soft,
    As soft as baby's skin."
The air closed over her words.
A firefly whirred near my ear, and in the distance
I could hear streetlamps ping
Into miniature suns
Against a feathery sky.

Adolescence—II

Although it is night, I sit in the bathroom, waiting.
Sweat prickles behind my knees, the baby-breasts are alert.
Venetian blinds slice up the moon; the tiles quiver in pale strips.

Then they come, the three seal men with eyes as round
As dinner plates and eyelashes like sharpened tines.
They bring the scent of licorice. One sits in the washbowl,

One on the bathtub edge; one leans against the door.
"Can you feel it yet?" they whisper.
I don't know what to say, again. They chuckle,

Patting their sleek bodies with their hands.
"Well, maybe next time." And they rise,
Glittering like pools of ink under moonlight,

And vanish. I clutch at the ragged holes
They leave behind, here at the edge of darkness.
Night rests like a ball of fur on my tongue.

Adolescence—III

With Dad gone, Mom and I worked
The dusky rows of tomatoes.
As they glowed orange in sunlight
And rotted in shadow, I too
Grew orange and softer, swelling out
Starched cotton slips.

The texture of twilight made me think of
Lengths of Dotted Swiss. In my room
I wrapped scarred knees in dresses
That once went to big-band dances;
I baptized my earlobes with rosewater.
Along the window-sill, the lipstick stubs
Glittered in their steel shells.

Looking out at the rows of clay
And chicken manure, I dreamed how it would happen:
He would meet me by the blue spruce,
A carnation over his heart, saying,
"I have come for you, Madam;
I have loved you in my dreams."
At his touch, the scabs would fall away.
Over his shoulder, I see my father coming toward us:
He carries his tears in a bowl,
And blood hangs in the pine-soaked air.

The Boast

At the dinner table, before the baked eggplant,
you tell the story of your friend, Ira,
how he kept a three-foot piranha in his basement.
"It was this long," you say, extending your arms,
"And it was striped, with silver scales and blue shadows."

The man with purple eyes lifts his eyebrows;
you laugh at his joke about the lady
in the sausage suit, your toes find his
under the table, and he is yours.

Evening expires in a yawn of stars.
But on the walk home,
when he pulls you into the hedges,
and the black tongues of leaves flutter,
and those boogy-man eyes glitter,
there won't be time for coming back
with lies, with lies.

The Kadava Kumbis Devise
a Way to Marry for Love

I will marry this clump of flowers
and throw it into the well!

There is no comfort in poverty.
"Better," they say, "to give yourself

to the soil under your feet
than to a man without jewels.

Who can feast off wind?"
So bring the gongs and the

old women—let us mourn
the loss of my youthful husband!

Where his frail hands paused
breath lingered, so that I am now

restless, a perfumed fan.
Who has suffered once

is not subject to pride.
I will marry again—perhaps to

that ragged man on the hill,
watching from a respectful distance.

Spy

She walked alone, as she did every morning.
Hers the narrow sidewalk, the corroded lamppost.
Larks thrilled the apricot air. Barbed crucifixes

Against the sky, the haloes of mist around streetlamps—
They reminded her of Jesus on a gilded altar
And Mama in a blue apron, praying.

Where were the oily midnights of depravity?
A woman of hard edges, blonde with dark armpits—
Where was she but always coming in from the cold?

First Kiss

And it was almost a boy who undid
the double sadness I'd sealed away.
He built a house in a meadow
no one stopped to admire,

and wore wrong clothes. Nothing
seemed to get in his way.
I promised him anything
if he would go. He smiled

and left. How
to re-create his motives,
irretrievable

as a gasp? Where else
to find him, counter-rising
in me, almost a boy. . . .

Then Came Flowers

I should have known if you gave me flowers
They would be chrysanthemums.
The white spikes singed my fingers.
I cried out; they spilled from the green tissue
And spread at my feet in a pool of soft fire.

If I begged you to stay, what good would it do me?
In the bed, you would lay the flowers between us.
I will pick them up later, arrange them with pincers.
All night from the bureau they'll watch me, their
Plumage as proud, as cocky as firecrackers.

Pearls

You have broken the path of the dragonfly
who visits my patio at the hour when
the sky has nearly forgotten the sun.
You have come to tell me
how happy we are, but I know
what you would and would not do
to make us happy. For example this necklace
before me: white eyes,
a noose of guileless tears.

Nexus

I wrote stubbornly into the evening.
At the window, a giant praying mantis
rubbed his monkey wrench head against the glass,
begging vacantly with pale eyes;

and the commas leapt at me like worms
or miniature scythes blackened with age.
The praying mantis screeched louder,
his ragged jaws opening onto formlessness.

I walked outside;
the grass hissed at my heels.
Up ahead in the lapping darkness
he wobbled, magnified and absurdly green,
a brontosaurus, a poet.

V

Notes from a Tunisian Journal

This nutmeg stick of a boy in loose trousers!
Little coffee pots in the coals, a mint on the tongue.

The camels stand in all their vague beauty—
at night they fold up like pale accordions.

All the hedges are singing with yellow birds!
A boy runs by with lemons in his hands.

Food's perfume, breath is nourishment.
The stars crumble, salt above eucalyptus fields.

The Sahara Bus Trip

I. *Departure*

Roofless houses, cartons of chalk,
catch the sky in their mirrors of air.
Intake of breath. Crisp
trees hung with sour oranges.
Hunched in the unnatural light, you wait
for the driver to start this bus forward.
Dust scatters in the pus-filled eyes
of children running after us, waving.
How small they are! They are getting smaller.

II. *The Discovery of Oranges*

At night they quiver imperceptibly until
the leaves rustle; their perforated skins
give off a faint heat.
Only the Arab knows the heart of the orange:
she tears herself apart to give us relief.
We spend 200 milliemes for a bag of oranges
so sweet our tongues lie dreaming in the juice.

III. *The Salt Sea*

If, at the end of the Atlantic,
Columbus had found only an absence of water,
this English tourist would have been there
to capture that void with a wide-angle lens.
Here, the wind blows from nowhere to nowhere
across a plain transformed by salt
into a vision of light. One bug,
black and white, dusted with salt, crawls
among orange peels that flare up like
brittle flowers. *You could not live here,*
he says. *It is not so astonishing,*
close your mouths.

IV. *The Discovery of Sandroses*

Each inconsolable thought sprouts
a tear of salt which blossoms,
sharpens into a razored petal.
Now we have a bouquet of stone roses.
The bedouins are hawking the new miracle,
600 milliemes, a few francs!
You buy me a large one.
By the roadside, the boys pose with foxes—
those diseased bastard eyes, those crumbling smiles.

V. *Hotel Nefta*

We disembark, the bus wheezing
like a punctured furnace.
The Englishman has set his tripod up
and is shooting the green interference of palms.
It is tricky light. Tomorrow the trip back,
our fingers exhaling small, tangy breaths.
What a light-hearted whistle you have!
It reminds me of water—so far-away,
so clear, it must come from the sky.

For Kazuko

The bolero, silk-tassled, the fuchsia
scarf come off: all that black hair

for the asking! You are unbraiding
small braids, your face full

behind a curtain of dark breath. Why
am I surprised when your lids emerge

from the fragrant paint? Now the couch
is baring its red throat, and now

you must understand me: your breasts,
so tiny, wound—or more precisely, echo

all the breasts which cannot swell, which
we prefer. I would like to lose myself

in those hushing thighs; but
sadness is not enough. A phallus

walks your dreams, Kazuko, lovely and
unidentified. Here is an anthology of wishes:

if fucking were graceful, desire an alibi.

Beauty and the Beast

Darling, the plates have been cleared away,
the servants are in their quarters.
What lies will we lie down with tonight?
The rabbit pounding in your heart, my

child legs, pale from a life of petticoats?
My father would not have had it otherwise
when he trudged the road home with our souvenirs.
You are so handsome it eats my heart away . . .

Beast, when you lay stupid with grief
at my feet, I was too young to see anything
die. Outside, the roses are folding
lip upon red lip. I miss my sisters—

they are standing before their clouded mirrors.
Gray animals are circling under the windows.
Sisters, don't you see what will snatch you up—
the expected, the handsome, the one who needs us?

His Shirt

does not show his
true colors. Ice-

blue and of stuff
so common

anyone
could have bought it,

his shirt
is known only

to me, and only
at certain times

of the day.
At dawn

it is a flag
in the middle

of a square
waiting to catch

chill light.
Unbuttoned, it's

a sail surprised
by boundless joy.

In candlelight at turns
a penitent's

scarf or beggar's
fleece, his shirt is

inapproachable.
It is the very shape

and tint
of desire

and could be mistaken
for something quite

fragile and
ordinary.

Great Uncle Beefheart

It was not as if he didn't try
to tell us: first he claimed
the velvet armchair, then the sun
on the carpet before it. Silence,
too, he claimed, although
we tried to spoil it with humming
and children's games. There was
that much charm left in the world.

It was not as if he didn't want
to believe us: he kept himself
neat. Behind his head, the anti-
macassar darkened, surrendered
the fragrance of bergamot.
Things creaked when he touched
them, so he stopped that, too.
He called us "dear little bugs,"

and it was not as if he
acted strange, though our mother
told her mother once
at least his heart was bigger
than any other man's.
That's when we called him
Great Uncle Beefheart; and it was not
as if he listened: he just

walked outdoors. Sunflowers,
wildly prosperous, took
the daylight and shook it
until our vision ran.
We found him in his shirtsleeves
in the onion patch, shivering
as he cried *I can't go back in
there, I ain't wearing no clothes.*

The Son

All the toothy Fräuleins are left behind:
blood machinery pumps the distance between you.
At the moment the landing gear
groans into the belly,
Mama's outside the window
in her shawl and her seed pearls.
She comes for help—your brother's
knocked down while restraining an inmate
and the family's counting on you . . .

A year ago Wagner sang you down the Rhine.
You stood in the failing light, certain
the Lorelei would toss you her comb.
Life could not bank and drop
you on the coal shores of Pittsburgh,
the house by factory light opening
its reluctant arms to boarders.

Corduroy Road

We strike camp on that portion of road completed
during the day. The strip of sky above me
darkens: this afternoon when it lurched into view
I felt air swoop down, and breathed it in.

Instruction:
Avoiding bogs and unduly rough terrain
Clear a track two rods wide
From Prairie du Chien to Fort Howard at Green Bay.

Today Carlton devised an interesting pastime.
From each trunk the axe has razed
a startled, upturned face awaits
refinement by the penknife:
The Jester. The Statesman. The Sot. The Maiden.

The symbol of motion is static, finite,
And kills by the coachload. Chances of perishing
On the road are ten to one, calculated
According to the following table of casualties:
1. By horses running away.
2. By overturning.
3. By drowning.
4. By murder.
5. By explosion.

Whenever a tree is felled, I think of a thousand blankets
ripped into sparks, or that the stillness itself
has been found and torn open with bare hands.
What prevails a man to hazard his person in the Wisconsin Forests
is closer to contrition than anything: the wild honey
blazing from outstretched palms, a skunk bagged and eaten in tears.

Ö

Shape the lips to an *o*, say *a*.
That's *island*.

One word of Swedish has changed the whole neighborhood.
When I look up, the yellow house on the corner
is a galleon stranded in flowers. Around it

the wind. Even the high roar of a leaf-mulcher
could be the horn-blast from a ship
as it skirts the misted shoals.

We don't need much more to keep things going.
Families complete themselves
and refuse to budge from the present,
the present extends its glass forehead to sea
(backyard breezes, scattered cardinals)

and if, one evening, the house on the corner
took off over the marshland,
neither I nor my neighbor
would be amazed. Sometimes

a word is found so right it trembles
at the slightest explanation.
You start out with one thing, end
up with another, and nothing's
like it used to be, not even the future.

MUSEUM

for nobody
who made us possible

I

The Hill Has Something to Say

Here lies
Ike Tell:
Heathen.
No chance of Heaven,
No fear of Hell.

—tombstone near
Weimar, Texas

The Fish in the Stone

The fish in the stone
would like to fall
back into the sea.

He is weary
of analysis, the small
predictable truths.
He is weary of waiting
in the open,
his profile stamped
by a white light.

In the ocean the silence
moves and moves

and so much is unnecessary!
Patient, he drifts
until the moment comes
to cast his
skeletal blossom.

The fish in the stone
knows to fail is
to do the living
a favor.

He knows why the ant
engineers a gangster's
funeral, garish
and perfectly amber.
He knows why the scientist
in secret delight
strokes the fern's
voluptuous braille.

The Ants of Argos

There stood the citadel—nothing left.
We climbed it anyway, if for no other reason
than to say we'd been someplace
where earth and air had been quietly
rearranged. Nothing was left

but you and me, standing above the small
and empty harbor flashing blue.
Around us wild thyme ached in mauve
and sun-baked stones fumed piquant
wherever shepherd boys had pissed

to hear them sizzle. Even the ants,
marching skyward, had been in Corinth.

Pithos

Climb
into a jar
and live
for a while.

Chill earth.
No stars
in this stone
sky.

You have ceased
to ache.

Your spine is
a flower.

Nestor's Bathtub

As usual, legend got it all
wrong: Nestor's wife was the one
to crouch under
jug upon jug of fragrant water poured
until the small room steamed.
But where was Nestor—
on his throne before the hearth,
counting the jars of oil
in storeroom 34, or
at the Trojan wars
while his wife with her white hands
scraped the dirt from a lover's back
with a bronze scalpel?

Legend, as usual, doesn't
say. But this heap of limestone
blocks—look how they fell, blasted
by the force of olive oil
exploding in the pot, look
at the pattern left in stucco
from the wooden columns, sixty
flutings, look at the shards
scattered in the hall where
jars spilled from the second floor,
oil spreading in flames
to the lady's throne.

For the sake of legend only the tub
stands, tiny and voluptuous
as a gravy dish.
And the blackened remains of ivory
combs and 2,853 tall-stemmed
drinking cups in the pantry—
these, too, survived
when the clay pots screamed
and stones sprang their sockets
and the olive trees grew into the hill.

The Hill Has Something to Say

but isn't talking.
Instead the valley groans as the wind,
amphoric,
hoots its one bad note.
Halfway up, we stop to peek
through smudged pine: this is Europe
and its green terraces.

≈

and takes its time.
What's left
to climb's inside us,
earth rising, stupified.

≈

: it's not all in the books
(but maps don't lie).
The hill has a right
to stand here, one knob
in the coiled spine of a peasant
who, forgetting to flee, simply
lay down forever.

≈

bootstrap and spur
harrow and pitchfork
a bugle a sandal
clay head of a pipe

≈

(For all we know
the wind's inside us, pacing
our lungs. For all we know
it's spring and the ground
moistens as raped maids break
to blossom. What's invisible
sings, and we bear witness.)

≈

if we would listen! Underfoot
slow weight, Scavenger Time,
and the little old woman
who lives there still.

The Copper Beech

Aristocrat among patriarchs, this
noble mutation is the best
specimen of Rococo

in the park of the castle
at Erpenberg.
The widely-traveled Baroness

returned
from a South American expedition
with any number of plants and a few

horticultural innovations.
This trailing beech became Erpenberg's
tree of grief, their

melancholy individualist,
the park philosopher.
Eight meters above lawn

the tousled crown
rises, her many plaited branches falling
like green water

earthwards, a cascade of leaves.
The aesthetic principles
of the period: branches

pruned late to heal
into knots, proud flesh ascending
the trunk:

living architecture.

Tou Wan Speaks to Her Husband, Liu Sheng

I will build you a house
of limited chambers
but it shall last
forever: four rooms
hewn in the side of stone
for you, my
only conqueror.

In the south room all
you will need for the journey
—a chariot, a
dozen horses—
opposite,

a figurine household
poised in servitude
and two bronze jugs, worth more
than a family pays in taxes
for the privilege to stay
alive, a year, together . . .

but you're bored.
Straight ahead then, the hall
leading to you, my
constant
emperor. Here
when the stench of your
own diminishing
drives you to air (but

you will find none), here
an incense burner
in the form of the mountain
around you, where hunters pursue
the sacred animal
and the peaks are drenched
in sun.

    For those times
in your niche when darkness
oppresses, I will set you
a lamp. (And a statue
of the palace girl you most
frequently coveted.)

And for your body,
two thousand jade wafers
with gold thread puzzled
to a brilliant envelope,
a suit to keep
the shape of your death—

when you are long light and clouds
over the earth, just as the legends prophesy.

Catherine of Alexandria

Deprived of learning and
   the chance to travel,
no wonder sainthood
   came as a voice

in your bed—
   and what went on
each night was fit
   for nobody's ears

but Jesus'. His
   breath of a lily.
His spiraling
   pain. Each morning

the nightshirt bunched
   above your waist—
a kept promise,
   a ring of milk.

Catherine of Siena

You walked the length of Italy
to find someone to talk to.
You struck the boulder at the roadside
since fate has doors everywhere.
Under the star-washed dome
of heaven, warm and dark

as the woolens stacked on cedar
shelves back home in your
father's shop, you prayed
until tears streaked the sky.
No one stumbled across your path.
No one unpried your fists as you slept.

Receiving the Stigmata

There is a way to enter a field
empty-handed, your shoulder
behind you and air tightening.

The kite comes by itself,
a spirit on a fluttering string.

Back when people died for
the smallest reasons, there was
always a field to walk into.
Simple men fell to their knees
below the radiant crucifix
and held out their palms

in relief. Go into the field
and it will reward. Grace

is a string growing straight
from the hand. Is
the hatchet's shadow on the
rippling green.

Boccaccio: The Plague Years

Even at night the air rang and rang.
Through the thick swirled glass
he watched the priests sweep past
in their peaked hoods, collecting death.
On each stoop a dish burning sweet
clotted smoke. He closed his eyes
to hear the slap
of flesh onto flesh, a
liquid crack like a grape
as it breaks on the tongue.

As a boy he had slipped
along the same streets, in love with
he didn't know whom. O the
reeded sonatinas and torch
flick on the chill slick sides
of the bridge and steam
rising in plumes
from the slaughterhouse vents—
twenty years.

Rolling out of the light
he leaned his cheek
against the rows of bound leather:
cool water. Fiammetta!
He had described her
a hundred ways; each time
she had proven unfaithful. If only
he could crack this city in two
so the moon would scour
the wormed streets clean! Or
walk away from it all, simply
falling in love again. . . .

Fiammetta Breaks Her Peace

I've watched them, mother, and I know
the signs. The first day, rigor.
Staggering like drunks, they
ram the room's sharp edges
with the most delicate bodily parts
and feel no pain. Unable
to sleep, they shiver beneath
all the quilts in the house,
panic gnawing a silver path to the brain.

Day two is fever, the bright
stream clogged, eyes rodent
red. No one weeps anymore; just
waits, for appear they must—
in the armpits, at the groin—
hard, blackened apples.
Then, at least, there is certainty,
an odd kind of relief;
a cross comes on the door.

A few worthy citizens gather possessions
around them and spend time
with fine foods, wine and music
behind closed drapes. Having left
the world already, they are surprised
when the world finds them again.
Still others carouse from tavern
to tavern, doing exactly as they please. . . .

And to think he wanted me
beautiful! To be his fresh air
and my breasts two soft
spiced promises. *Stand still,* he said
once, *and let me admire you.*

All is infection, mother—and avarice,
and self-pity, and fear!
We shall sit quietly in this room,
and I think we'll be spared.

II

In the Bulrush

When the morning
gather the rainbow,
want you to know
I'm a rainbow, too.

—*Bob Marley*

November for Beginners

Snow would be the easy
way out—that softening
sky like a sigh of relief
at finally being allowed
to yield. No dice.
We stack twigs for burning
in glistening patches
but the rain won't give.

So we wait, breeding
mood, making music
of decline. We sit down
in the smell of the past
and rise in a light
that is already leaving.
We ache in secret,
memorizing

a gloomy line
or two of German.
When spring comes
we promise to act
the fool. Pour,
rain! Sail, wind,
with your cargo of zithers!

Reading Hölderlin on the Patio
with the Aid of a Dictionary

One by one, the words
give themselves
up, white flags dispatched
from a silent camp.

When had my shyness returned?

This evening, the sky refused
to lie down. The sun crouched
behind leaves, but the trees
had long since walked away.
The meaning that surfaces

comes to me aslant and
I go to meet it, stepping
out of my body
word for word, until I am

everything at once: the perfume
of the world in which
I go under,
a skindiver
remembering air.

Shakespeare Say

He drums the piano wood,
crowing.

Champion Jack in love
and in debt,
in a tan walking suit
with a flag on the pocket,
with a red eye
for women, with a
diamond-studded
ear, with sand
in a mouthful of mush—

poor me
poor me
I keep on drifting
like a ship out
on the sea

That afternoon two students
from the Akademie
showed him the town.
Munich was misbehaving,
whipping
his ass to ice
while his shoes
soaked through. His guides
pointed at a clock
in a blue-tiled house.
And tonight

every song he sings
is written by Shakespeare
and his mother-in-law.
I love you, baby,
but it don't mean
a goddam thing.
In trouble
with every woman he's
ever known, all of them
ugly—skinny legs, lie gap
waiting behind the lips
to suck him in.

Going down slow
crooning *Shakespeare say*
man must be
careful what he kiss
when he drunk,
going down
for the third set
past the stragglers
at the bar,
the bourbon in his hand
some bitch's cold
wet heart,
the whole joint

stinking on beer;
in love and winning
now, so even the mistakes
sound like jazz,
poor me, moaning
so no one hears:

my home's in Louisiana,
my voice is wrong,
I'm broke and can't hold
my piss;
my mother told me
there'd be days like this.

Three Days of Forest, a River, Free

The dogs have nothing better
to do than bark; duty's whistle
slings a bright cord
around their throats.
I'll stand here all night
if need be, no more real
than a tree when no moon shines.

The terror of waking is a trust
drawn out unbearably
until nothing, not even love,
makes it easier, and yet
I love this life:

three days of forest,
the mute riot of leaves.

Who can point out a smell
but a dog? The way is free
to the river. Tell me,
Lord, how it feels
to burst out like a rose.

Blood rises in my head—
I'm there.
Faint tongue, dry fear,
I think I lost you to the dogs,
so far off now they're no
more than a chain of bells
ringing darkly, underground.

Banneker

What did he do except lie
under a pear tree, wrapped in
a great cloak, and meditate
on the heavenly bodies?
Venerable, the good people of Baltimore
whispered, shocked and more than
a little afraid. After all it was said
he took to strong drink.
Why else would he stay out
under the stars all night
and why hadn't he married?

But who would want him! Neither
Ethiopian nor English, neither
lucky nor crazy, a capacious bird
humming as he penned in his mind
another enflamed letter
to President Jefferson— he imagined
the reply, polite and rhetorical.
Those who had been to Philadelphia
reported the statue
of Benjamin Franklin
before the library

his very size and likeness.
A wife? No, thank you.
At dawn he milked
the cows, then went inside
and put on a pot to stew
while he slept. The clock
he whittled as a boy
still ran. Neighbors
woke him up
with warm bread and quilts.
At nightfall he took out

his rifle— a white-maned
figure stalking the darkened
breast of the Union— and
shot at the stars, and by chance
one went out. Had he killed?
I assure thee, my dear Sir!
Lowering his eyes to fields
sweet with the rot of spring, he could see
a government's domed city
rising from the morass and spreading
in a spiral of lights. . . .

In the Bulrush

Cut a cane that once
grew in the river.
Lean on it. Weigh

a stone in your hands
and put it down again.
Watch it moss over.

Strike the stone
to see if it's thinking
of water.

Delft

Flat, with variations. Not
the table but the cloth.
As if a continent
raging westward, staggered
at the sight of
so much water, sky
on curdling sky.

Wherever I walk
the earth's soft
mouth suckles.
These clumps of beeches,
glazed trunks
green with age.
Each brick house the original
oven, fired to stay
incipient mold,

while in the hour
of least resolve
the starched sheets
scratch the insomniac wife
to bravado. *At least,*
she whispers,

we dine in style.
And our sceneries
please. We may be standing
on a porch
open to the world
but the house behind us
is sinking.

Ike

Grew hair for fun.
Found a mouth harp.
Scared away the bees.

The creek and the ford
Built step by step.
Sassy finch: kept time
To his creaking knee.

Up the hill fine
Families benched
And wailing. Organ
Panting, a diseased
Lung.

Marched outback.
Shot a cottonmouth.

Heard it twitch
The whole night long.

Agosta the Winged Man
and Rasha the Black Dove

Schad paced the length of his studio
and stopped at the wall,

                staring

at a blank space. Behind him
the clang and hum of Hardenbergstrasse, its
automobiles and organ grinders.

                          Quarter to five.

His eyes traveled
to the plaster scrollwork
on the ceiling. Did *that*

                  hold back heaven?

He could not leave his skin— once
he'd painted himself in a new one,
silk green, worn
like a shirt.

          He thought

of Rasha, so far from Madagascar,
turning slowly in place as
the boa constrictor
coiled counterwise its

                 heavy love. How

the spectators gawked, exhaling
beer and sour herring sighs.
When the tent lights dimmed,
Rasha went back to her trailer and plucked
a chicken for dinner.

               The canvas,

not his eye, was merciless.
He remembered Katja the Russian

aristocrat, late
for every sitting,
                      still fleeing
the October Revolution—
how she clutched her sides
and said not
                one word. Whereas Agosta
(the doorbell rang)
was always on time, lip curled
as he spoke in wonder of women
                                    trailing
backstage to offer him
the consummate bloom of their lust.

Schad would place him
on a throne, a white sheet tucked
over his loins, the black suit jacket
thrown off like a cloak.
Agosta had told him
                      of the medical students
at the Charité,
that chill arena
                   where he perched on
a cot, his torso
exposed, its crests and fins
a colony of birds, trying
to get out . . .
                and the students,
lumps caught
in their throats, taking notes.

Ah, Rasha's
           foot on the stair.
She moved slowly, as if she carried
the snake around her body
always.

                    Once
she brought fresh eggs into
the studio, flecked and
warm as breath.
                    Agosta in
classical drapery, then,
and Rasha at his feet.
Without passion. Not
the canvas
              but their gaze,
              so calm,
was merciless.

At the German Writers Conference in Munich

In the large hall of the Hofbräuhaus
above the heads of the members
of the board, taut and white
as skin (not mine),
tacked across a tapestry
this banner:

Association of German
Writers in the Union of Printers
and Paper Manufacturers.

Below it some flowers,
typical medieval,
and a maiden's feet
under a printed silk gown.
The tapestry pokes out

all over: a woman
in a green kerchief,
a king with a scepter and
crown puffed like a soufflé;
an ash-blonde princess
by birthright permitted
to bare her crinklets
to sun and smoke. Then another
lady-in-waiting, this time
in a white kerchief
and a white horse craning
to observe the royal party.

At the bottom strip of needlework
four flat bread loaves.
Far in the eaves
two doves signify
a union endorsed
by God and the Church.
Further, green hills
rolling with pine.

Above them all a banner
unfurled and inscribed
in Latin. Maybe it says
Association of Tapestrers
in the Union of Wives
and Jewish Dyers.
No one's feet are visible
but those dainty shoes
beneath the printed silk
that first caught my eye,
and the grotesquely bent
fetlock-to-ivory hoof
of the horse. And both
are in flowers.

III

My Father's Telescope

Then I went an' stood up
On some high ol' lonesome hill
I went an' stood up
On some high ol' lonesome hill
An' looked down on the house
Where I used to live

—*Bessie Smith*

Grape Sherbet

The day? Memorial.
After the grill
Dad appears with his masterpiece—
swirled snow, gelled light.
We cheer. The recipe's
a secret and he fights
a smile, his cap turned up
so the bib resembles a duck.

That morning we galloped
through the grassed-over mounds
and named each stone
for a lost milk tooth. Each dollop
of sherbet, later,
is a miracle,
like salt on a melon that makes it sweeter.

Everyone agrees— it's wonderful!
It's just how we imagined lavender
would taste. The diabetic grandmother
stares from the porch,
a torch
of pure refusal.

We thought no one was lying
there under our feet,
we thought it
was a joke. I've been trying
to remember the taste,
but it doesn't exist.
Now I see why
you bothered,
father.

Roses

It's time you learned something.
Halfway outdoors
he pauses, the flat dark fury of
his jaw, one eye, a shoulder in torn
blue cloth, the pruning shears
a mammoth claw resting
between meals.

        I scramble
up, terrified and down
the drive, the gravel's
brittle froth
and stand completely
helpless as he parts
a thousand pinkish eyelids
to find the beetles nested
at the root, teeming
disease.

They came from Japan, 1961.
They were nothing like the locusts
we hadn't noticed until they
were gone, the husks
sheer tuxedos
snagged on bark, the rafters,
the dying bayberry.

It's easy—
pop them between your nails.
In the tool shed's populous
shadows, I hold the Mason jar instead
with both hands as he shakes
the flowers above
the kerosene which is shivering now
like the ocean I have never seen . . .

and I bear on a tray indoors
the inculpable, blushing prize.

Sunday Night at Grandfather's

He liked to joke and all of his jokes were practical.
The bent thumb jiggling between two ribs, his
Faked and drunken swoon. We tipped by and
He caught us, grandfather's right, right
Up to the cliff of his pure white
Shirt, real Fruit-of-the-
Loom. We shrieked and
He cackled like
A living
Ghost.

He hated Billy the parakeet, mean as half-baked sin.
He hated church-going women and the radio turned
Up loud. His favorite son, called Billy
Too, had flown the coop although
Each year he visited, each
Time from a different
City, gold
Tooth and
Drunk.

Then out came the cherry soda and potato chips and pretzels.
Grandma humming hymns and rocking in the back bedroom.
Dad holding Billy out on a thick and bitten finger,
Saying *Here: Come on Joe—touch him.*
Every Sunday night the same.
Dad's quiet urging and
That laugh: *You've*
Got to be
Kidding,
Son.

Centipede

With the storm moved on the next town
we take a flashlight down to the basement

Nested chairs stripped of varnish
Turpentine shadows stiff legs in the air

Look by the fusebox a centipede Dad says
I scream and let go of his hairy arm

My Father's Telescope

The oldest joke
in the world,
a chair on three legs.

Sawdust kicks
up, swirls
around his boots

and settles
in the cuffs of his
pants. The saw is

as nervous as
a parrot.
The chair

shrinks. After
years of cupboards
and end tables, after

a plywood Santa
and seven elves
for the lawn in snow,

he knows.
He's failed, and
in oak.

Next Christmas
he buys himself
and his son

a telescope.

Song. Summer

Sexless, my brother flies
over the house. He is glad
to have this dark vegetable
taken from him and hums

as he circles. The air
brims; already forgotten
his name and the beckoning
shapes below on the lawn.

In the evening my brother
dips, a dark cross fluttering.
He hears the eaves
murmur; he watches the open

mouth of my father. Now
he smiles, sailing
over the roof, heading
straight for the blue cloud

of pine.

Anti-Father

Contrary to
tales you told us

summer nights when
the air conditioner

broke—the stars
are not far

apart. Rather
they draw

closer together
with years.

And houses
shrivel, un-lost,

and porches sag;
neighbors phone

to report cracks
in the cellar floor,

roots of the willow
coming up. Stars

speak to a child.
The past

is silent. . . .
Just between

me and you,
woman to man,

outer space is
inconceivably

intimate.

To Bed

We turn off
the light and
walk upstairs.
Scurrile moon
and a crazed
sniper hugging
the roof, a nickel
and its buffalo.
The house is
strange, the screen
padlocked
for luck, for
riches, for
love, the cup
of water in my
hands dark
as a well.
Dark swells. The
last one up
is the first
to go.

A Father out Walking
on the Lawn

Five rings light your approach across
the dark. You're lonely, anyone

can tell— so many of you
trembling, at the center the thick

dark root. Out here on a lawn
twenty-one years
gone under the haunches of a neighbor's

house, American Beauties
lining a driveway the mirror image of your own,

you wander, waiting to be
discovered. What
can I say to a body
that merely looks

like you? The willow, infatuated with its
surroundings, quakes; not that violent
orgasm nor the vain promise of

a rose relinquishing
its famous scent all for you, no,

not even the single
brilliant feather

a blue jay loses in flight
which dangles momentarily, azure scimitar,
above the warm eaves of your house—
nothing can change

this travesty, this
magician's skew of scarves
issuing from an opaque heart.

Who sees you anyway, except
at night, and with a fantastic eye?

If only you were bright enough to touch!

IV

Primer for the Nuclear Age

> Doc, all my life people say
> I was ugly. (pause) Makes me
> feel mean.
>
> —*Boris Karloff,*
> *in* The Raven

The Sailor in Africa

a Viennese card game, circa 1910

There are two white captains
and two Moors. The pilots complement
their superiors, while the crew,
eight hands per master, wear
identical motley.
Available also, four ships
and a wild card
(starburst) which
luck can change into
a schooner or
a beautiful woman.

The captains, pilots, crews
commence
from the globe's four
corners. They share
a sun, a moon, and one
treasure. The goal
is Africa. One must uphold
the proportions between
superior and subordinate
while obtaining
chips. There are several cards
representing either
cannons or cannonballs
to make matters more
interesting. Plus a pair
of dice, for where
can we go without chance?

Say the Italian Moor
sails in sunshine
to Morocco and is rewarded
five black chips. Meanwhile
the British captain and
his swarthy pilot are stranded
with an overladen ship
somewhere between the Ibos and
Jamestown, Virginia.
The moon intrudes. When
the Spanish brigantine looms
on the horizon, they are actually
grateful, for they have cannons
and the Sevillian does not.

Both ships proceed
to Virginia. The arrow swings
east. Monsieur de la Roque
parades on deck, a small
white anchor stitched
on a blue field over
his heart. He surveys
his craft, finely strung
as a harp. *If all goes well
we'll reach Santo Domingo
tomorrow. . . .*

By now the Italian vessel
is safely through
the Suez Canal,
but a card shows "gale"
and it runs aground
on the western shore
of Madagascar, miraculously
unscathed. The captain falls
asleep on the beach, dreaming

of gold. Awake, he finds
ship and crew vanished, the
sun grinning and the treasure
secure at the bottom of the deck.
—Will he,

           like the Spanish Moor,
be sold, merchant
to merchandise, or will
wild boars discover
him first? Monsieur de la Roque
has landed at Santo Domingo,
picking up rum and a slave
named Pedro. Such
flashing eyes and refined
manners! He'll make
an excellent valet.

Adrift in the Atlantic
again, the Englishman
plays quoits with his pilot,
his eyes raw
from staring into the sun.
A desperate man, he will
choose the beautiful woman
and die.

        While Pedro— who,
it turns out, is none other
than the Captain from Seville,
has loosened the leg irons
and drugged the fastidious
de la Roque! Now the
white anchor heaves
on the breast of the Moor, and
the sun beams on the mutinous

crew of his brother, who have
cleared the Cape of
Good Hope and are bearing
down on the Guinea coast.
Pedro heads

for Brazil— the women there,
he's heard, are prodigious!
Then the arrow swerves
due south, "gale" shows
from nowhere, the treasure
drops to the ocean floor.
At the sight of so many
mountains surging
whitely ahead, a crew hand,
thinking he has gone
to hell, falls
overboard, his red sash
flaring. Even

Pedro, lashed to the mast,
believes he has glimpsed
through the storm's
pearly membrane
God's dark face swooping
down to kiss— as the main
sail, incandescent under
pressure, bursts
like a star. The ship
splinters
on the rocks

　　　　　just as, deep
in the Madagascan forests,
a black hand

lifts from a nest
an egg the bright
green of malachite. . . .

At least one man happy
to have lost everything.
His crew will make it home
with tales of strange lands
and their captain's untimely
demise.

In the Atlantic,
windstill.
The English vessel, so
close to home, stalls.
Nothing for them to do
but pass the time
playing cards.

Early Morning
on the Tel Aviv–Haifa Freeway

The shore is cabbage green and reeks.
Reclaimed swamp sprouts citrus
and tamarisk, manna to the ancients
who were starved for miracles.
Now a paper mill and Alliance Tires
spill their secrets further out to sea.

Along the roadside, two Arab boys
drag a gull by the wings
and beyond a horse belly-up in the field.
A glider dips over us, silent, and
gleams as it turns. We should stop
but drive on.

Why I Turned Vegetarian

Mister Minister, I found
the tip of your thumb
bit off a way back:
a neat cap. Begging
your pardon, perhaps
you'd miss it
sooner or later.
You probably dropped it
folding the newspaper.

I don't mean to intrude.
I saw no other way less painful
or designed. It was lying
where I couldn't fail
to spot it— still fresh
with color and ridges
and a sliver of nail
and the teeth marks
showing— the only
edible mushroom
in the whole plot of grass.

Eastern European Eclogues

I

This melodious
prison: crowds
shivering around
the sausage stalls.

II

One of us will
suffer. Don't move.
Not one word
more. You're
imagining things.

III

All that's quiet
is magic. Fields
steaming with dung.
Fresh meat in the air.

IV

One of us will need
a month in the country
to ward off imminent
complications.

V

Who?
Of course not.
Why should they.
Of course not.

VI

The countryside
is lovely
this time of year

Flirtation

After all, there's no need
to say anything

at first. An orange, peeled
and quartered, flares

like a tulip on a wedgwood plate.
Anything can happen.

Outside the sun
has rolled up her rugs

and night strewn salt
across the sky. My heart

is humming a tune
I haven't heard in years!

Quiet's cool flesh—
let's sniff and eat it.

There are ways
to make of the moment

a topiary
so the pleasure's in

walking through.

Exeunt the Viols

with their throb and yearn, their sad
stomach of an alley cat. Listen:

even the ocean mourns the passage
of voices so pure and penetrant, that

insect hum. Who discovered usefulness?
Who forgot how to sing, simply?

(Magnificence spoke up briefly, followed
by the race boat's break-neck

dazzle.) A tremor rises in the throat
of the cat, the quill jerks in the hand

of the melancholy scribe. The gambas
beat a retreat, gracefully—

their last chord a breath drawn
deep in a garden maze, there

near the statue
smiling under the stars.

The Left-Handed Cellist

You came with a cello in one hand,
in the other, nothing.
Play, you said.

I played the scales of ignorant evenings.
I played in high heels to be closer to you.

When you snapped off a stem
from the vase, you broke
my little finger.

This is a theme in mauve:
it begins with the children's blind bodies,
it ends with the boys in the orchestra.

Tell me that you did not profit from me,
you with the pewter hands.

Lines Muttered in Sleep

Black chest hairs, soft sudden mass.
Washed up on her breast his pale and startled face.
Pine scent, lake scent, gorse scent, bark.

Primer for the Nuclear Age

At the edge of the mariner's
  map is written: "Beyond
  this point lie Monsters."

Someone left the light on
  in the pantry—there's
  a skull in there on the shelf

that talks. Blue eyes
  in the air, blue as
  an idiot's. Any fear, any

memory will do; and if you've
  got a heart at all, someday
  it will kill you.

Parsley

1. *The Cane Fields*

There is a parrot imitating spring
in the palace, its feathers parsley green.
Out of the swamp the cane appears

to haunt us, and we cut it down. El General
searches for a word; he is all the world
there is. Like a parrot imitating spring,

we lie down screaming as rain punches through
and we come up green. We cannot speak an R—
out of the swamp, the cane appears

and then the mountain we call in whispers *Katalina*.
The children gnaw their teeth to arrowheads.
There is a parrot imitating spring.

El General has found his word: *perejil*.
Who says it, lives. He laughs, teeth shining
out of the swamp. The cane appears

in our dreams, lashed by wind and streaming.
And we lie down. For every drop of blood
there is a parrot imitating spring.
Out of the swamp the cane appears.

2. *The Palace*

The word the general's chosen is parsley.
It is fall, when thoughts turn
to love and death; the general thinks
of his mother, how she died in the fall
and he planted her walking cane at the grave
and it flowered, each spring stolidly forming
four-star blossoms. The general

pulls on his boots, he stomps to
her room in the palace, the one without
curtains, the one with a parrot
in a brass ring. As he paces he wonders
Who can I kill today. And for a moment
the little knot of screams
is still. The parrot, who has traveled

all the way from Australia in an ivory
cage, is, coy as a widow, practising
spring. Ever since the morning
his mother collapsed in the kitchen
while baking skull-shaped candies
for the Day of the Dead, the general
has hated sweets. He orders pastries
brought up for the bird; they arrive

dusted with sugar on a bed of lace.
The knot in his throat starts to twitch;
he sees his boots the first day in battle
splashed with mud and urine
as a soldier falls at his feet amazed—
how stupid he looked!— at the sound
of artillery. *I never thought it would sing*
the soldier said, and died. Now

the general sees the fields of sugar
cane, lashed by rain and streaming.
He sees his mother's smile, the teeth
gnawed to arrowheads. He hears
the Haitians sing without R's
as they swing the great machetes:
Katalina, they sing, *Katalina*,

mi madle, mi amol en muelte. God knows
his mother was no stupid woman; she
could roll an R like a queen. Even
a parrot can roll an R! In the bare room
the bright feathers arch in a parody
of greenery, as the last pale crumbs
disappear under the blackened tongue. Someone

calls out his name in a voice
so like his mother's, a startled tear
splashes the tip of his right boot.
My mother, my love in death.
The general remembers the tiny green sprigs
men of his village wore in their capes
to honor the birth of a son. He will
order many, this time, to be killed

for a single, beautiful word.

Notes

Tou Wan Speaks to Her Husband, Liu Sheng: Liu Sheng, Prince Ching of Chung Shan, died in 113 B.C. He and his wife lived in the middle of the Western Han Dynasty. Their tombs were unearthed west of Mancheng, Hopei Province, in 1968.

Catherine of Alexandria: (died 307?). She rebuked the Roman emperor Galerius Valerius Maximinus, who then condemned her to be broken on the wheel. The wheel miraculously disintegrated.

Catherine of Siena: (1347–1380). A wool merchant's daughter, Catherine refused to marry. She received the stigmata and worked to secure peace between the Papacy and a divided Italy, dictating letters of advice to people all over Europe.

Shakespeare Say: Champion Jack Dupree, black American blues singer, toured extensively in Europe.

Banneker: Benjamin Banneker (1731–1806), first black man to devise an almanac and predict a solar eclipse accurately, was also appointed to the commission that surveyed and laid out what is now Washington, D.C.

Agosta the Winged Man and Rasha the Black Dove: Christian Schad (1894–1982) painted the two sideshow entertainers in Berlin in 1929.

Parsley: On October 2, 1957, Rafael Trujillo (1891–1961), dictator of the Dominican Republic, ordered 20,000 blacks killed because they could not pronounce the letter "r" in *perejil,* the Spanish word for parsley.

THOMAS

AND

BEULAH

*These poems tell two sides of a story
and are meant to be read in sequence.*

I

Mandolin

Black Boy, O Black Boy,
is the port worth the cruise?

—*Melvin B. Tolson,*
Harlem Gallery

The Event

Ever since they'd left the Tennessee ridge
with nothing to boast of
but good looks and a mandolin,

the two Negroes leaning
on the rail of a riverboat
were inseparable: Lem plucked

to Thomas' silver falsetto.
But the night was hot and they were drunk.
They spat where the wheel

churned mud and moonlight,
they called to the tarantulas
down among the bananas

to come out and dance.
*You're so fine and mighty; let's see
what you can do,* said Thomas, pointing

to a tree-capped island.
Lem stripped, spoke easy: *Them's chestnuts,
I believe.* Dove

quick as a gasp. Thomas, dry
on deck, saw the green crown shake
as the island slipped

under, dissolved
in the thickening stream.
At his feet

a stinking circle of rags,
the half-shell mandolin.
Where the wheel turned the water

gently shirred.

Variation on Pain

Two strings, one pierced cry.
So many ways to imitate
The ringing in his ears.

He lay on the bunk, mandolin
In his arms. Two strings
For each note and seventeen
Frets; ridged sound
Humming beneath calloused
Fingertips.

There was a needle
In his head but nothing
Fit through it. Sound quivered
Like a rope stretched clear
To land, tensed and brimming,
A man gurgling air.

Two greased strings
For each pierced lobe:
So is the past forgiven.

Jiving

Heading North, straw hat
cocked on the back of his head,

tight curls gleaming
with brilliantine, he didn't stop

until the nights of chaw
and river-bright

had retreated, somehow
into another's life. He landed

in Akron, Ohio
1921,

on the dingy beach
of a man-made lake.

Since what he'd been through
he was always jiving, gold hoop

from the right ear jiggling
and a glass stud, bright blue

in his left. The young ladies
saying *He sure plays*

that tater bug
like the devil!

sighing their sighs
and dimpling.

Straw Hat

In the city, under the saw-toothed leaves of an oak
overlooking the tracks, he sits out
the last minutes before dawn, lucky
to sleep third shift. Years before
he was anything, he lay on
so many kinds of grass, under stars,
the moon's bald eye opposing.

He used to sleep like a glass of water
held up in the hand of a very young girl.
Then he learned he wasn't perfect, that
no one was perfect. So he made his way
North under the bland roof of a tent
too small for even his lean body.

The mattress ticking he shares in the work barracks
is brown and smells
from the sweat of two other men.
One of them chews snuff:
he's never met either.
To him, work is a narrow grief
and the music afterwards
is like a woman
reaching into his chest
to spread it around. When he sings

he closes his eyes.
He never knows when she'll be coming
but when she leaves, he always
tips his hat.

Courtship

1.

Fine evening may I have
the pleasure . . .
up and down the block
waiting—for what? A
magnolia breeze, someone
to trot out the stars?

But she won't set a foot
in his turtledove Nash,
it wasn't proper.
Her pleated skirt fans
softly, a circlet of arrows.

King of the Crawfish
in his yellow scarf,
mandolin belly pressed tight
to his hounds-tooth vest—
his wrist flicks for the pleats
all in a row, sighing . . .

2.

. . . so he wraps the yellow silk
still warm from his throat
around her shoulders. (He made
good money; he could buy another.)
A gnat flies
in his eye and she thinks
he's crying.

Then the parlor festooned
like a ship and Thomas
twirling his hat in his hands
wondering how did I get here.
China pugs guarding a fringed settee
where a father, half-Cherokee,
smokes and frowns.
I'll give her a good life—
what was he doing,
selling all for a song?
His heart fluttering shut
then slowly opening.

Refrain

The man inside the mandolin
plays a new tune
every night, sailing
past the bedroom window:

Take a gourd and string it
Take a banana and peel it
Buy a baby blue Nash
And wheel and deal it

Now he's raised a mast
and tied himself to it
with rags, drunker
than a robin on the wing:

Count your kisses
Sweet as honey
Count your boss'
Dirty money

The bed's oak
and clumsy, pitching
with its crew,
a man and a wife—

Now he's dancing, moving
only his feet. No way
to shut him up but
roll over, scattering

ruffles and silk,
stiff with a dog's breath
among lilies
and ripening skin:

Love on a raft
By the light o' the moon
And the bandit gaze
Of the old raccoon.

Variation on Guilt

Count it anyway he wants—
by the waiting room clock,
by a lengthening hangnail,
by his buttons, the cigars crackling
in cellophane—

no explosion. No latch clangs
home. Perfect bystander, high
and dry with a scream caught
in his throat, he looks down

the row of faces coddled
in anxious pride. Wretched
little difference, he thinks,
between enduring pain and
waiting for pain
to work on others.

The doors fly apart—no,
he wouldn't run away!
It's a girl, he can tell
by that smirk, that strut of a mountebank!

But he doesn't feel a thing.
Weak with rage,
Thomas deals the cigars,
spits out the bitter tip in tears.

Nothing Down

He lets her pick the color.
She saunters along the gleaming fenders
trying to guess his mind.

> *The flower*
> *dangled, blue flame*
> *above his head.*
> *He had stumbled into the woods*
> *and found this silent*
> *forgiveness.*

How they'd all talk!
Punkin and Babe,
Willemma tsk-tsking in her
sinking cabin,

> *a child's forest,*
> *moss and threads*
> *gone wild with hope*

the boys down by the creek
grown now, straddling
the rail at the General Store . . .

> *Lem smiled from a tree*
> *and nodded when Thomas told him*
> *he was a few years early.*
> *"We'll run away together,"*
> *was all Lem said.*

She bends over,
admiring her reflection
in the headlamp casing of a Peerless.

On an ordinary day
he would have plucked this
blue trumpet of Heaven
and rushed it home to water.

"Nigger Red,"
she drawls, moving on.

"Catching a woman," Lem used
to say, "is like rubbing
two pieces of silk together.
Done right, the sheen jags
and the grit shines through."

A sky blue Chandler!
She pauses, feeling his gaze.

Every male on the Ridge
old enough to whistle
was either in the woods
or under a porch.
He could hear the dogs
rippling up the hill.

Eight miles outside Murfreesboro
the burn of stripped rubber,
soft mud of a ditch.
A carload of white men
halloo past them on Route 231.
"You and your South!" she shouts
above the radiator hiss.
"Don't tell me this ain't what
you were hoping for."

The air was being torn
into hopeless pieces.
Only this flower hovering
above his head
couldn't hear the screaming.
That is why the petals had grown
so final.

The Zeppelin Factory

The zeppelin factory
needed workers, all right—
but, standing in the cage
of the whale's belly, sparks
flying off the joints
and noise thundering,
Thomas wanted to sit
right down and cry.

That spring the third
largest airship was dubbed
the biggest joke
in town, though they all
turned out for the launch.
Wind caught,
"The Akron" floated
out of control,

three men in tow—
one dropped
to safety, one
hung on but the third,
muscles and adrenalin
failing, fell
clawing
six hundred feet.

Thomas at night
in the vacant lot:
> Here I am, intact
> and faint-hearted.

Thomas hiding
his heart with his hat
at the football game, eyeing
the Goodyear blimp overhead:
> *Big boy I know*
> *you're in there.*

Under the Viaduct, 1932

He avoided the empty millyards,
the households towering
next to the curb. It was dark
where he walked, although above him
the traffic was hissing.

He poked a trail in the mud
with his tin-capped stick.
If he had a son this time
he would teach him how to step
between his family and the police,
the mob bellowing
as a kettle of communal soup
spilled over a gray bank of clothes. . . .

The pavement wobbled, loosened by rain.
He liked it down here
where the luck of the mighty
had tumbled,

black suit and collarbone.
He could smell the worms stirring in their holes.
He could watch the white sheet settle
while all across the North Hill Viaduct

tires slithered to a halt.

Lightnin' Blues

On the radio a canary bewailed her luck
while the county outside was kicking with rain.
The kids bickered in the back seat;
the wife gasped whenever lightning struck
where it damn well pleased. Friday night,

and he never sang better. The fish
would be flashing like beautiful sequined cigars.
This time he'd fixed the bait himself,
cornmeal and a little sugar water
stirred to a ball on the stove,
pinched off for the scavenger carp.

So why did the car stall? And leap
backwards every time he turned the key?
Was Gabriel a paper man, a horn player
who could follow only the notes on the score?
Or was this sheriff the culprit,
pressing his badge to the window to say
You're lucky—a tree fell on the road ahead
just a few minutes ago.

Turned around, the car started
meek as a lamb. No one spoke
but that old trickster on the radio,
Kingfish addressing the Mystic Knights of the Sea.

Compendium

He gave up fine cordials and
his hounds-tooth vest.

He became a sweet tenor
in the gospel choir.

Canary, usurper
of his wife's affections.

Girl girl
girl girl.

In the parlor, with streamers,
a bug on a nail.

The canary courting its effigy.
The girls fragrant in their beds.

Definition in the Face of Unnamed Fury

That dragonfly, bloated, pinned
to the wall, its gossamer wings in tatters
(yellow silk, actually, faded in rivulets)—
what is it? A pendulum
with time on its hands, a frozen
teardrop, a winter melon
with a white, sweet flesh?

Go on—ask the canary.
Ask that sun-bleached delicacy
in its house of sticks
and it will answer *Pelican's bill.*
What else did you expect?

"How long has it been . . . ?"
Too long. Each note slips
into querulous rebuke, fingerpads
scored with pain, shallow ditches
to rut in like a runaway slave
with a barking heart. Days afterwards
blisters to hide from the children.
Hanging by a thread. *Some day,*
he threatens, *I'll just
let go.*

Aircraft

Too frail for combat, he stands
before an interrupted wing,
playing with an idea, nothing serious.
Afternoons, the hall gaped with aluminum
glaring, flying toward the sun; now
though, first thing in the morning, there is only
gray sheen and chatter
from the robust women around him
and the bolt waiting for his riveter's
five second blast.

The night before in the dark
of the peanut gallery, he listened to blouses shifting
and sniffed magnolias, white
tongues of remorse
sinking into the earth. Then
the newsreel leapt forward
into war.

Why *frail*? Why not simply
family man? Why wings, when
women with fingers no smaller than his
dabble in the gnarled intelligence of an engine?

And if he gave just a four second blast,
or three? Reflection is such

a bloodless light.
After lunch, they would bathe in fire.

Aurora Borealis

This far south such crippling
Radiance. People surge
From their homes onto the streets, certain
This is the end,
For it is 1943
And they are tired.

Thomas walks out of the movie house
And forgets where he is.
He is drowning and
The darkness above him
Spits and churns.

What shines is a thought
Which has lost its way. Helpless
It hangs and shivers
Like a veil. So much

For despair.
Thomas, go home.

Variation on Gaining a Son

That shy angle of his daughter's head—
where did they all learn it?
And her soldier at tender attention,
waiting for the beloved to slide out
beneath the veil. Thomas knew

what he'd find there—a mocking smile, valiant
like that on the smooth face of the young sergeant
drilled neatly through the first minute of battle.
Women called it *offering up a kiss*.

He watched the bridegroom swallow.
For the first time Thomas felt like
calling him *Son*.

One Volume Missing

Green sludge of a riverbank,
swirled and blotched,
as if a tree above him were shuffling
cards.
      Who would have thought
the binding of a "Standard Work
of Reference in the Arts,
Science, History, Discovery
and Invention" could bring back

slow afternoons with a line and bent nail

here, his wingtips balanced
on a scuffed linoleum square
at the basement rummage sale
of the A.M.E. Zion Church?

He opens *Motherwell-Orion* and finds
orchids on the frontispiece
overlain with tissue,
fever-specked and drooping
their enflamed penises.

Werner's Encyclopedia,
Akron, Ohio, 1909:
Complete in Twenty-Five Volumes
minus one—

for five bucks
no zebras, no Virginia,
no wars.

The Charm

They called us
the tater bug twins.
We could take a tune
and chew it up, fling
it to the moon
for the crows to eat.

At night he saw him,
naked and swollen
under the backyard tree.
No reason, he replied
when asked why he'd done
it. Thomas woke up
minutes later, thinking
What I need is a drink.

Sunday mornings
fried fish and hominy steaming
from the plates like an oracle.
The canary sang more furious
than ever, but he heard
the whisper: *I ain't dead.*
I just gave you my life.

Gospel

Swing low so I
can step inside—
a humming ship of voices
big with all

the wrongs done
done them.
No sound this generous
could fail:

ride joy until
it cracks like an egg,
make sorrow
seethe and whisper.

From a fortress
of animal misery
soars the chill voice
of the tenor, enraptured

with sacrifice.
What do I see,
he complains, notes
brightly rising

towards a sky
blank with promise.
Yet how healthy
the single contralto

settling deeper
into her watery furs!
Carry me home,
she cajoles, bearing

down. Candelabras
brim. But he slips
through God's net and swims
heavenward, warbling.

Roast Possum

The possum's a greasy critter
that lives on persimmons and what
the Bible calls carrion.
So much from the 1909 Werner
Encyclopedia, three rows of deep green
along the wall. A granddaughter
propped on each knee,
Thomas went on with his tale—

but it was for Malcolm, little
Red Delicious, that he invented
embellishments: *We shined that possum*
with a torch and I shinnied up,
being the smallest,
to shake him down. He glared at me,
teeth bared like a shark's
in that torpedo snout.
Man he was tough but no match
for old-time know-how.

Malcolm hung back, studying them
with his gold hawk eyes. When the girls
got restless, Thomas talked horses:
Strolling Jim, who could balance
a glass of water on his back
and trot the village square
without spilling a drop. Who put
Wartrace on the map and was buried
under a stone, like a man.

They liked that part.
He could have gone on to tell them
that the Werner admitted Negro children
to be intelligent, though briskness
clouded over at puberty, bringing
indirection and laziness. Instead,
he added: *You got to be careful*
with a possum when he's on the ground;
he'll turn on his back and play dead
till you give up looking. That's
what you'd call sullin'.

Malcolm interrupted to ask
who owned Strolling Jim,
and who paid for the tombstone.
They stared each other down
man to man, before Thomas,
as a grandfather, replied:
                    Yessir,
we enjoyed that possum. We ate him
real slow, with sweet potatoes.

The Stroke

Later he'll say Death stepped right up
to shake his hand, then squeezed
until he sank to his knees. *(Get up,*
nigger. Get up and try again.)

Much later he'll admit he'd been afraid,
curled tight in the center of the rug, sunlight
striking one cheek and plaited raffia
scratching the other. He'll leave out

the part about daydream's aromatic fields
and the strap-worn flanks of the mule
he followed through them. When his wife asks
how did it feel, he won't mention

that the sun shone like the summer
she was pregnant with their first, and
that she craved watermelon which he smuggled
home wrapped in a newspaper, and how

the bus driver smirked as his nickel
clicked through—no, he'll say
it was like being kicked by a mule.
Right now, though, pinned to the bull's-eye,

he knows it was Lem all along:
Lem's knuckles tapping his chest in passing,
Lem's heart, for safekeeping,
he shores up in his arms.

The Satisfaction Coal Company

1.

What to do with a day.
Leaf through *Jet*. Watch T.V.
Freezing on the porch
but he goes anyhow, snow too high
for a walk, the ice treacherous.
Inside, the gas heater takes care of itself;
he doesn't even notice being warm.

Everyone says he looks great.
Across the street a drunk stands smiling
at something carved in a tree.
The new neighbor with the floating hips
scoots out to get the mail
and waves once, brightly,
storm door clipping her heel on the way in.

2.

Twice a week he had taken the bus down Glendale hill
to the corner of Market. Slipped through
the alley by the canal and let himself in.
Started to sweep
with terrible care, like a woman
brushing shine into her hair,
same motion, same lullaby.
No curtains—the cop on the beat
stopped outside once in the hour
to swing his billy club and glare.

It was better on Saturdays
when the children came along:
he mopped while they emptied
ashtrays, clang of glass on metal
then a dry scutter. Next they counted

nailheads studding the leather cushions.
Thirty-four! they shouted,
that was the year and
they found it mighty amusing.

But during the week he noticed more—
lights when they gushed or dimmed
at the Portage Hotel, the 10:32
picking up speed past the B & O switchyard,
floorboards trembling and the explosive
kachook kachook kachook kachook
and the oiled rails ticking underneath.

3.

They were poor then but everyone had been poor.
He hadn't minded the sweeping,
just the thought of it—like now
when people ask him what he's thinking
and he says *I'm listening*.

Those nights walking home alone,
the bucket of coal scraps banging his knee,
he'd hear a roaring furnace
with its dry, familiar heat. Now the nights
take care of themselves—as for the days,
there is the canary's sweet curdled song,
the wino smiling through his dribble.
Past the hill, past the gorge
choked with wild sumac in summer,
the corner has been upgraded.
Still, he'd like to go down there someday
to stand for a while, and get warm.

Thomas at the Wheel

This, then, the river he had to swim.
Through the wipers the drugstore
shouted, lit up like a casino,
neon script leering from the shuddering asphalt.

Then the glass doors flew apart
and a man walked out to the curb
to light a cigarette. Thomas thought
the sky was emptying itself as fast
as his chest was filling with water.

Should he honk? What a joke—
he couldn't ungrip the steering wheel.
The man looked him calmly in the eye
and tossed the match away.

And now the street dark, not a soul
nor its brother. He lay down across
the seat, a pod set to sea,
a kiss unpuckering. He watched
the slit eye of the glove compartment,
the prescription inside,

he laughed as he thought *Oh
the writing on the water*. Thomas imagined
his wife as she awoke missing him,
cracking a window. He heard sirens
rise as the keys swung, ticking.

II

Canary in Bloom

Ah, how the senses flood at my repeating,
As once in her fire-lit heart I felt the furies
Beating, beating.

—Anne Spencer,
"Lines to a Nasturtium"

Taking in Wash

Papa called her Pearl when he came home
drunk, swaying as if the wind touched
only him. Towards winter his skin paled,
buckeye to ginger root, cold drawing
the yellow out. The Cherokee in him,
Mama said. Mama never changed:
when the dog crawled under the stove
and the back gate slammed, Mama hid
the laundry. Sheba barked as she barked
in snow or clover, a spoiled and ornery bitch.

She was Papa's girl,
black though she was. Once,
in winter, she walked through a dream
all the way down the stairs
to stop at the mirror, a beast
with stricken eyes
who screamed the house awake. Tonight

every light hums, the kitchen arctic
with sheets. Papa is making the hankies
sail. Her foot upon a silk
stitched rose, she waits
until he turns, his smile sliding all over.
Mama a tight dark fist.
Touch that child

and I'll cut you down
just like the cedar of Lebanon.

Magic

Practice makes perfect, the old folks said.
So she rehearsed deception
until ice cubes
dangled willingly
from a plain white string
and she could change
an egg into her last nickel.
Sent to the yard to sharpen,

she bent so long over
the wheel the knives
grew thin. When she stood up,
her brow shorn clean
as a wheatfield and
stippled with blood,
she felt nothing, even
when Mama screamed.

She fed sauerkraut to the apple tree;
the apples bloomed tarter
every year. Like all art
useless and beautiful, like
sailing in air,

things happened
to her. One night she awoke
and on the lawn blazed
a scaffolding strung in lights.
Next morning the Sunday paper
showed the Eiffel Tower
soaring through clouds.
It was a sign

she would make it to Paris one day.

Courtship, Diligence

A yellow scarf runs through his fingers
as if it were melting.
Thomas dabbing his brow.

And now his mandolin in a hurry
though the night, as they say,
is young,
though she is *getting on*.

Hush, the strings tinkle. *Pretty gal.*

Cigar-box music!
She'd much prefer a pianola
and scent in a sky-colored flask.

Not that scarf, bright as butter.
Not his hands, cool as dimes.

Promises

Each hurt swallowed
is a stone. Last words
whispered to his daughter
as he placed her fingertips
lightly into the palm
of her groom.

She smiled upwards
to Jesus, then Thomas,
turning her back as
politely as possible.
If that were the case
he was a mountain of shame.

Poised on the stone
steps of the church,
she tried to forget
his hulk in the vestibule,
clumsy in blue serge,
his fingers worrying the
lucky bead in his pocket.

Beneath the airborne bouquet
was a meadow of virgins
urging *Be water, be light.*
A deep breath, and she plunged
through sunbeams and kisses,
rice drumming
the both of them blind.

Dusting

Every day a wilderness—no
shade in sight. Beulah
patient among knicknacks,
the solarium a rage
of light, a grainstorm
as her gray cloth brings
dark wood to life.

Under her hand scrolls
and crests gleam
darker still. What
was his name, that
silly boy at the fair with
the rifle booth? And his kiss and
the clear bowl with one bright
fish, rippling
wound!

Not Michael—
something finer. Each dust
stroke a deep breath and
the canary in bloom.
Wavery memory: home
from a dance, the front door
blown open and the parlor
in snow, she rushed
the bowl to the stove, watched
as the locket of ice
dissolved and he
swam free.

That was years before
Father gave her up
with her name, years before
her name grew to mean
Promise, then
Desert-in-Peace.
Long before the shadow and
sun's accomplice, the tree.

Maurice.

A Hill of Beans

One spring the circus gave
free passes and there was music,
the screens unlatched
to let in starlight. At the well,
a monkey tipped her his fine red hat
and drank from a china cup.
By mid-morning her cobblers
were cooling on the sill.
Then the tents folded and the grass

grew back with a path
torn waist-high to the railroad
where the hoboes jumped the slow curve
just outside Union Station.
She fed them while they talked,
easy in their rags. *Any two points
make a line,* they'd say,
and we're gonna ride them all.

Cat hairs
came up with the dipper;
Thomas tossed on his pillow
as if at sea. When money failed
for peaches, she pulled
rhubarb at the edge of the field.
Then another man showed up
in her kitchen and she smelled
fear in his grimy overalls,
the pale eyes bright as salt.

There wasn't even pork
for the navy beans. But he ate
straight down to the blue
bottom of the pot and rested
there a moment, hardly breathing.
That night she made Thomas
board up the well.
Beyond the tracks, the city blazed
as if looks were everything.

Weathering Out

She liked mornings the best—Thomas gone
to look for work, her coffee flushed with milk,

outside autumn trees blowsy and dripping.
Past the seventh month she couldn't see her feet

so she floated from room to room, houseshoes flapping,
navigating corners in wonder. When she leaned

against a door jamb to yawn, she disappeared entirely.

Last week they had taken a bus at dawn
to the new airdock. The hangar slid open in segments

and the zeppelin nosed forward in its silver envelope.
The men walked it out gingerly, like a poodle,

then tied it to a mast and went back inside.
Beulah felt just that large and placid, a lake;

she glistened from cocoa butter smoothed in
when Thomas returned every evening nearly

in tears. He'd lean an ear on her belly
and say: *Little fellow's really talking,*

though to her it was more the *pok-pok-pok*
of a fingernail tapping a thick cream lampshade.

Sometimes during the night she woke and found him
asleep there and the child sleeping, too.

The coffee was good but too little. Outside
everything shivered in tinfoil—only the clover

between the cobblestones hung stubbornly on,
green as an afterthought. . . .

Motherhood

She dreams the baby's so small she keeps
misplacing it—it rolls from the hutch
and the mouse carries it home, it disappears
with his shirt in the wash.
Then she drops it and it explodes
like a watermelon, eyes spitting.

Finally they get to the countryside;
Thomas has it in a sling.
He's strewing rice along the road
while the trees chitter with tiny birds.
In the meadow to their right three men
are playing rough with a white wolf. She calls

warning but the wolf breaks free
and she runs, the rattle
rolls into the gully, then she's
there and tossing the baby behind her,
listening for its cry as she straddles
the wolf and circles its throat, counting
until her thumbs push through to the earth.
White fur seeps red. She is hardly breathing.
The small wild eyes
go opaque with confusion and shame, like a child's.

Anniversary

Twelve years to the day
he puts the blue worry bead into his mouth.
The trick is to swallow your good luck, too.
Last words to a daughter . . .
and a wink to remember him by.

The House on Bishop Street

No front yard to speak of,
just a porch cantilevered on faith
where she arranged the canary's cage.
The house stayed dark all year
though there was instant light and water.
(No more gas jets hissing,

their flicker glinting off
Anna Rettich's midwife spectacles
as she whispered *think a baby*
and the babies came.) Spring
brought a whiff of cherries, the kind
you boiled for hours in sugar and cloves

from the yard of the Jewish family next door.
Yumanski refused to speak so
she never bought his vegetables
at the Canal Street Market. Gertrude,
his youngest and blondest,
slipped by mornings for bacon and grits.
There were summer floods and mildew

humming through fringe, there was
a picture of a ship she passed
on her way to the porch, strangers calling
from the street *Ma'am, your bird
shore can sing!* If she leaned out she could glimpse
the faintest of mauve—no more than an idea—
growing just behind the last houses.

Daystar

She wanted a little room for thinking:
but she saw diapers steaming on the line,
a doll slumped behind the door.

So she lugged a chair behind the garage
to sit out the children's naps.

Sometimes there were things to watch—
the pinched armor of a vanished cricket,
a floating maple leaf. Other days
she stared until she was assured
when she closed her eyes
she'd see only her own vivid blood.

She had an hour, at best, before Liza appeared
pouting from the top of the stairs.
And just *what* was mother doing
out back with the field mice? Why,

building a palace. Later
that night when Thomas rolled over and
lurched into her, she would open her eyes
and think of the place that was hers
for an hour—where
she was nothing,
pure nothing, in the middle of the day.

Obedience

That smokestack, for instance,
in the vacant lot across the street:
if she could order it down and watch
it float in lapse-time over buckled tar and macadam
it would stop an inch or two perhaps
before her patent leather shoes.

Her body's no longer tender, but her mind is free.
She can think up a twilight, sulfur
flicking orange then black
as the tip of a flamingo's wing, the white
picket fence marching up the hill . . .

but she would never create such puny stars.
The house, shut up like a pocket watch,
those tight hearts breathing inside—
she could never invent them.

The Great Palaces of Versailles

Nothing nastier than a white person!
She mutters as she irons alterations
in the backroom of Charlotte's Dress Shoppe.
The steam rising from a cranberry wool
comes alive with perspiration
and stale Evening of Paris.
Swamp she born from, swamp
she swallow, swamp she got to sink again.

The iron shoves gently
into a gusset, waits until
the puckers bloom away. Beyond
the curtain, the white girls are all
wearing shoulder pads to make their faces
delicate. That laugh would be Autumn,
tossing her hair in imitation of Bacall.

Beulah had read in the library
how French ladies at court would tuck
their fans in a sleeve
and walk in the gardens for air. Swaying
among lilies, lifting shy layers of silk,
they dropped excrement as daintily
as handkerchieves. Against all rules

she had saved the lining from a botched coat
to face last year's gray skirt. She knows
whenever she lifts a knee
she flashes crimson. That seems legitimate;
but in the book she had read
how the *cavaliere* amused themselves
wearing powder and perfume and spraying
yellow borders knee-high on the stucco
of the *Orangerie.*

A hanger clatters
in the front of the shoppe.
Beulah remembers how
even Autumn could lean into a settee
with her ankles crossed, sighing
I need a man who'll protect me
while smoking her cigarette down to the very end.

Pomade

She sweeps the kitchen floor of the river bed her husband saw fit
to bring home with his catfish, recalling
a flower—very straight,
with a spiked collar arching
under a crown of bright fluffy worms—
she had gathered in armfuls
along a still road in Tennessee. Even then
he was forever off in the woods somewhere in search
of a magic creek.

It was Willemma shushed the pack of dusty children
and took her inside the leaning cabin with its little
window in the door, the cutout magazine cloud taped to the pane
so's I'll always have shade. It was Willemma
showed her how to rub the petals fine
and heat them slow in mineral oil
until the skillet exhaled pears and nuts and rotting fir.

That cabin leaned straight away
to the south, took the very slant of heaven
through the crabgrass and Queen Anne's Lace to
the Colored Cemetery down in Wartrace. Barley soup
yearned toward the bowl's edge, the cornbread
hot from the oven climbed in glory
to the very black lip of the cast iron pan . . .
but Willemma stood straight as the day
she walked five miles to town for Scotch tape
and back again. Gaslight flickered on the cockeyed surface
of rain water in a galvanized pail in the corner
while Thomas pleaded with his sister
to get out while she still was fit.

Beebalm. The fragrance always put her
in mind of Turkish minarets against
a sky wrenched blue,
sweet and merciless. Willemma could wear her gray hair twisted
in two knots at the temples and still smell like travel.
But all those years she didn't budge. She simply turned
one day from slicing a turnip into a pot
when her chest opened and the inrushing air
knocked her down. *Call the reverend, I'm in the floor*
she called out to a passerby.

Beulah gazes through the pale speckled linoleum
to the webbed loam with its salt and worms. She smooths
her hair, then sniffs her palms. On the countertop
the catfish grins
like an oriental gentleman. Nothing ever stops. She feels
herself slowly rolling down the sides of the earth.

Headdress

The hat on the table
in the dining room
is no pet trained
to sit still. Three
pearl-tipped spears and Beulah
maneuvering her shadow
to the floor. The hat
is cold. The hat
wants more.

(The customer will be
generous when satisfied
beyond belief. Spangled
tulle, then, in green
and gold and sherry.)

Beulah
would have settled
for less. She doesn't
pray when she's
terrified, sometimes, in-
side her skin like
today, humming
through a mouthful of pins.

Finished it's a mountain
on a dish, a capitol
poised on a littered shore.
The brim believes   .
in itself, its
double rose and feathers
ashiver. Extravagance
redeems. O
intimate parasol
that teaches to walk
with grace along beauty's seam.

Sunday Greens

She wants to hear
wine pouring.
She wants to taste
change. She wants
pride to roar through
the kitchen till it shines
like straw, she wants

lean to replace
tradition. Ham knocks
in the pot, nothing
but bones, each
with its bracelet
of flesh.

The house stinks
like a zoo in summer,
while upstairs
her man sleeps on.
Robe slung over
her arm and
the cradled hymnal,

she pauses, remembers
her mother in a slip
lost in blues,
and those collards,
wild-eared,
singing.

Recovery

He's tucked his feet into corduroy scuffs
and gone out to the porch. From the parlor
with its glassed butterflies, the mandolin on the wall,
she can see one bare heel bobbing.

Years ago he had promised to take her to Chicago.
He was lovely then, a pigeon
whose pulse could be seen when the moment
was perfectly still. In the house

the dark rises and whirrs like a loom.
She stands by the davenport,
obedient among her trinkets,
secrets like birdsong in the air.

Nightmare

She's dreaming
of salt again:
salt stinging her eyes,
making pepper of her hair,
salt in her panties
and the light all over.
If she wakes
she'll find him
gone and the dog
barking its tail off,
locked outside in the
dead of night.

Lids pinched shut,
she forces the itching
away. That streetlamp
through the window:
iridescent grit. As a girl
she once opened
an umbrella in the house
and her mother cried
you'll ruin us!
but that was so
long ago. Then
she wakes up.

Wingfoot Lake

(Independence Day, 1964)

On her 36th birthday, Thomas had shown her
her first swimming pool. It had been
his favorite color, exactly—just
so much of it, the swimmers' white arms jutting
into the chevrons of high society.
She had rolled up her window
and told him to drive on, fast.

Now this *act of mercy*: four daughters
dragging her to their husbands' company picnic,
white families on one side and them
on the other, unpacking the same
squeeze bottles of Heinz, the same
waxy beef patties and Salem potato chip bags.
So he was dead for the first time
on Fourth of July—ten years ago

had been harder, waiting for something to happen,
and ten years before that, the girls
like young horses eyeing the track.
Last August she stood alone for hours
in front of the T.V. set
as a crow's wing moved slowly through
the white streets of government.
That brave swimming

scared her, like Joanna saying
Mother, we're Afro-Americans now!
What did she know about Africa?
Were there lakes like this one
with a rowboat pushed under the pier?
Or Thomas' Great Mississippi
with its sullen silks? (There was
the Nile but the Nile belonged

to God.) Where she came from
was the past, 12 miles into town
where nobody had locked their back door,
and Goodyear hadn't begun to dream of a park
under the company symbol, a white foot
sprouting two small wings.

Company

No one can help him anymore.
Not the young thing next door
in the red pedal pushers,
not the canary he drove distracted

with his mandolin. There'll be
no more trees to wake him in moonlight,
nor a single dry spring morning
when the fish are lonely for company.

She's standing there telling him: give it up.
She is weary of sirens and his face
worn with salt. *If this is code,*

she tells him, *listen: we were good,*
though we never believed it.
And now he can't even touch her feet.

The Oriental Ballerina

twirls on the tips of a carnation
while the radio scratches out a morning hymn.
Daylight has not ventured as far

as the windows—the walls are still dark,
shadowed with the ghosts
of oversized gardenias. The ballerina

pirouettes to the wheeze of the old
rugged cross, she lifts
her shoulders past the edge

of the jewelbox lid. Two pink slippers
touch the ragged petals, no one
should have feet that small! In China

they do everything upside down:
this ballerina has not risen but drilled
a tunnel straight to America

where the bedrooms of the poor
are papered in vulgar flowers
on a background the color of grease, of

teabags, of cracked imitation walnut veneer.
On the other side of the world
they are shedding robes sprigged with

roses, roses drifting with a hiss
to the floor by the bed
as, here, the sun finally strikes the windows

suddenly opaque,
noncommital as shields. In this room
is a bed where the sun has gone

walking. Where a straw nods over
the lip of its glass and a hand
reaches for a tissue, crumpling it to a flower.

The ballerina has been drilling all night!
She flaunts her skirts like sails,
whirling in a disk so bright,

so rapidly she is standing still.
The sun walks the bed to the pillow
and pauses for breath (in the Orient,

breath floats like mist
in the fields), hesitating
at a knotted handkerchief that has slid

on its string and has lodged beneath
the right ear which discerns
the most fragile music

where there is none. The ballerina dances
at the end of a tunnel of light,
she spins on her impossible toes—

the rest is shadow.
The head on the pillow sees nothing
else, though it feels the sun warming

its cheeks. *There is no China;*
no cross, just the papery kiss
of a kleen·x above the stink of camphor,

the walls exploding with shabby tutus. . . .

Chronology

1900:	Thomas born in Wartrace, Tennessee.
1904:	Beulah born in Rockmart, Georgia.
1906:	Beulah's family moves to Akron.
1916:	30,000 workers migrate to Akron.
1919:	Thomas leaves Tennessee for the riverboat life.
1921:	Thomas arrives in Akron.
1922:	Completion of viaduct spanning the Little Cuyahoga River.
1924:	December wedding.
1926:	First child born (Rose).
1928:	New car bought for the trip to Tennessee.
1929:	The Goodyear Zeppelin Airdock is built—the largest building in the world without interior supports.
1930:	Lose car due to the Depression. Second child born (Agnes).
1931:	The airship *Akron* disaster.
1932:	Vice-President of First Central Trust Company commits suicide. A union organizer is killed trying to aid an evicted family.
1932:	November: Third child born (Liza).
1934:	Part-time work cleaning offices of the Satisfaction Coal Company.
1935:	Fourth child born (Joanna). They move to Bishop Street.
1940:	11,000 Negroes living in Akron (total population: 243,000).

1942:   Thomas employed at Goodyear Aircraft in war relief work.

1945:   Rose marries a war veteran.

1946:   Thomas quits the gospel choir at the A.M.E. Zion Church.

1946:   Beulah takes a part-time job in Charlotte's Dress Shoppe.

1947:   First grandchild (Pauline) born to Rose.

1949:   Second grandchild (Jacqueline) born to Rose.

1950:   Beulah takes up millinery.

1951:   The only grandson (Malcolm) born to Agnes.

1956:   All daughters have been married off.

1960:   Thomas has first heart attack.

1963:   End of July: Thomas dies.

1963:   August: The March on Washington.

1964:   Beulah's daughters invite her to a Fourth of July picnic.

1966:   Beulah afflicted with glaucoma. She takes to her bed.

1969:   April: Beulah dies.

Index of Titles

Acknowledgments

The Yellow House on the Corner

Some of these poems have appeared in the following magazines and anthologies:

Antaeus, The American Poetry Anthology, Eating the Menu, Georgia Review, Intro 6, Miami Alumni, Missouri Review, New Honolulu Review, North American Review, Ohio Review, Paris Review, Pearl, Prairie Schooner, Snapdragon, Three Rivers Poetry Journal, and *The Virginia Quarterly Review.*

"Nigger Song: An Odyssey," "Adolescence—II," and "Planning the Perfect Evening" appeared originally in *Antaeus.* "Robert Schumann, or: Musical Genius Begins with Affliction" and "Small Town" appeared originally in *The Georgia Review.* "Adolescence—III" is reprinted from *Prairie Schooner,* Vol. 49, No. 1 by permission of University of Nebraska Press. Copyright © 1975 by University of Nebraska Press. "The Boast" by Rita Dove from *Intro 6,* edited by George Garrett. Copyright © 1974 by Associated Writing Programs. Reprinted by permission of Doubleday & Company, Inc.

Museum

Some of these poems have appeared in the following magazines:

The Georgia Review: "The Hill Has Something to Say," "Receiving the Stigmata"; *Kenyon Review:* "Grape Sherbet"; *Massachusetts Review:* "Anti-Father," "Three Days of Forest, a River, Free"; *The Nation:* "The Ants of Argos"; *National Forum:* "The Fish in the Stone"; *New Orleans Review:* "The Left-Handed Cellist"; *Ontario Review:* "Eastern European Eclogues," "Parsley"; *Poetry:* "Agosta the Winged Man and Rasha the Black Dove," "Dusting," "November for Beginners" (© 1981 Modern Poetry Association), "Flirtation" (© 1982 Modern Poetry Association); *Poetry NOW:* "Lines Muttered in Sleep," "Tou Wan Speaks to Her Husband, Liu Sheng"; *The Reaper:* "At the German Writers Conference in Munich," "Primer for the Nuclear Age," "Shakespeare Say"; *Tesseract:* "Catherine of Alexandria," "Catherine of Siena," "Reading Hölderlin on the Patio with the Aid of a Dictionary."

The quote at the beginning of section II ("In the Bulrush") is from the song "Sun is shining" by Bob Marley. © 1977 Bob Marley Music Ltd. Used by permission.

Thomas and Beulah

These poems have appeared, sometimes in different versions, in the following magazines:

Acknowledgments

Agni Review: "Daystar," "Weathering Out"; *Callaloo:* "Company," "The House on Bishop Street," "Motherhood," "Nightmare," "One Volume Missing," "Promises," "Recovery," "Roast Possum," "Straw Hat," "Under the Viaduct, 1932"; *Cutbank:* "Aircraft," "Obedience"; *Georgia Review:* "Gospel"; *New England Review & Bread Loaf Quarterly:* "Courtship, Diligence," "The Oriental Ballerina"; *Nimrod:* "Magic," "Sunday Greens"; *Paris Review:* "Lightnin' Blues," "The Satisfaction Coal Company," "Wingfoot Lake"; *Ploughshares:* "Taking in Wash"; *Poetry:* "Pomade"; *The Reaper:* "A Hill of Beans," "Nothing Down," "Thomas at the Wheel."

The following poems appeared as a chapbook feature under the title *Mandolin* in *Ohio Review 28:* "The Event," "Variation on Pain," "Jiving," "The Zeppelin Factory," "Courtship," "Refrain," "Variation on Guilt," "Compendium," "Definition in the Face of Unnamed Fury," "Aurora Borealis," "The Charm," and "The Stroke."

"The Great Palaces of Versailles," "Pomade," and "The Oriental Ballerina" appeared in *New American Poets of the Eighties* (Wampeter Press, 1984). "Dusting" first appeared in *Poetry* and subsequently in *Pushcart Prize: VII* (Pushcart Press, 1982), *Museum* (Carnegie-Mellon University Press, 1983), and *The Morrow Anthology of Younger American Poets* (1985).

"A Hill of Beans" and "Wingfoot Lake" also appeared in *The Bread Loaf Anthology of Contemporary American Poetry* (University Press of New England, 1985).

Rita Dove was born and raised in Akron, Ohio. She has published the novel *Through the Ivory Gate,* a collection of stories, and four previous books of poetry, among them *Thomas and Beulah,* which was awarded the Pulitzer Prize in 1987. Other honors include fellowships from the National Endowment for the Arts and the Guggenheim Foundation. Commonwealth Professor of English at the University of Virginia, she lives in Charlottesville with her husband, Fred Viebahn, and their daughter, Aviva. In 1993, Ms. Dove was named Poet Laureate of the United States.